This book is a must-read if…

- you are stuck in a rut

- you like real-life stories

- you are looking for an adventure

- you are looking for inspiration

- you are considering a journey of self-discovery

- you are curious to know what it takes to step outside your comfort zone

- you want to learn what it takes to seize the day

- you want a funny and light-hearted read

- you want to live a whole and fulfilling life

- you are looking for the female equivalent of Bill Bryson

When opportunity comes knocking,
grab it with both hands...

The Impulsive Explorer

One businesswoman's accidental journey
of self-discovery on an expedition
to the Antarctic

Karen Espley

First published in Great Britain in 2021
by Book Brilliance Publishing
265A Fir Tree Road, Epsom, Surrey, KT17 3LF
+44 (0)20 8641 5090
www.bookbrilliancepublishing.com
admin@bookbrilliancepublishing.com

A CIP catalogue record for this book is available
at the British Library.

ISBN 978-1-913770-08-2.
Typeset in Myriad Pro.
Printed by IngramSpark.

This book is a memoir. It reflectstheauthor'spresentrecollections
of experiences over time. Some names and characteristics have
been changed, some events have been compressed,
and some dialogue has been recreated.

Every efforthasbeenmadetocontactthepeopleinthismemoir.
The publisher would be delighted to correct any omissions
in future editions.

Dedication

For those who dare to dream…

'*The Impulsive Explorer* is instantly relatable for anyone of a certain age who's ever been caught in the corporate rat trap and dreamt of a better life. Filled with gentle humour (and the occasional rip roaring belly laugh), it's a book that's underscored with both profound personal insights and universal truths about the fragility of humanity as a whole and of each of us as individuals. At the same time, *The Impulsive Explorer* will awaken even the most dormant of wanderlusts and gently nudges those of us who lack Espley's courage to step out of our comfort zones and into a life of adventure.'

– Lucy Pitts
Editor, *Sussex Exclusive*

'An unputdownable book! Rather like a box of chocolates, you want to finish it all in one go. Highly recommended reading for the armchair adventurer.'

– Sue Stockdale
First UK woman to ski to the Magnetic North Pole

'*The Impulsive Explorer* is about bravery, of not letting arbitrary limits diminish your potential and opportunities, and living your life to its fullest. Karen demonstrates more bravery and chutzpah than 99% of the UK population. It's a bloody good adventure showing that sometimes you just have to JFDI.'

– Andrew Middleton
Founder of INDY (I'm Not Done Yet)

'A storming ride that grips you from the beginning. A true quest of self-discovery, with a spot of adventure that shows great strength of character, coupled with a soupçon of derring-do. Absorbing from beginning to end.'

– Geoff Douglass

'Few are fortunate of a perfect childhood and adolescence; Karen's was no exception which makes this story all the more inspirational. It made me introspective about my upbringing and showed the constraints that I still hold today.

If you're familiar with the corporate world, you'll recognise the being chewed up and spat out – but Karen demonstrates it's possible to escape from the "golden handcuffs" of that world.

The pictures that Karen conjures of the Antarctic are vivid, not just the scenery and the natural (and "unnatural"!) inhabitants but also of the pollution and how we're very slowly trying to put it right.

A cry, then laugh, then cheer story.'

– Ian Challand

'Gripping and honest dive into the life of a super-dooper-modest woman with loads to give.'

– Spoon The Voice Guy (spoonsvoices.com)

'Karen Espley guides us on her journey starting from a shaky childhood, via the freedom of university and into the corporate chasm of the 1990s. We follow our impulsive explorer as she stands full height (all 5'2" of it) and faces childhood trauma, depression and sexism to head off on the adventure she'd always dreamt of.

As she joins a research trip to Antarctica, Karen's descriptive writing and humour brings to life the colourful characters she meets along the way, together with the bleak Russian base camp, partying with the Uruguayans, pizza fuelled nights of salsa dancing and encounters with smelly penguins, angry sea lions and ferocious skuas. The confined living quarters, different personalities and difficult group dynamics are balanced by stunning scenery, once in a lifetime events and wonderful memories shared from what was clearly a life altering experience.

I had the privilege of reading this delightfully honest and exhilarating tale before publication and Karen's friendly tone as she describes her physical and mental journey makes it feel as though you're with an old friend, it's one of those books you want to read from beginning to end in one glorious go.'

– Laura Stokes
Cheltenham Lifestyle & Business

Contents

Foreword

by Robert Swan, OBE, BA, FRGS

Raised in Yorkshire, England, Robert Swan is the first person in history to walk to both the North and South Poles. After seeing first-hand the effects of climate change, Robert has dedicated himself to protecting Antarctica and our planet at large. Positive participation and a committed team have enabled Robert to educate and stimulate people across the globe.

I first met Karen Espley at the beginning of 2000 before she set off on the One Step Beyond, Mission Antarctica Expedition to King George Island in the Antarctic Peninsula. The aim of this expedition was to support a Russian team at the Bellingshausen Base that was collecting all of the waste around the base for extraction and removal within the following couple of years.

Karen was very enthusiastic about the project; in fact, I would go as far as to say she was rather overexcited. She reminded me of the Andrex puppy with her boundless energy as she chatted away, hoping to impress me with the amount of research she had done in readiness for the trip. You will understand this charming image as you read through the pages of *The Impulsive Explorer*.

Early on in this gripping and funny book, you will learn about Karen's challenging early years. Her story immediately draws you into her world and demonstrates her resilience when faced with challenges. Exactly the characteristics needed for a journey to the outskirts of civilisation. An example of which was when the voyage was put in jeopardy early on, when the *Vavilov* (the ship that took them across the Drake Passage) broke down and they had to return to Ushuaia.

Karen's enthusiasm for the expedition as a whole was evident in the additional environmental project she undertook; testing out a new kit for the Water Research Council. In the book, you can see the maps that Karen drew as part of the data gathering needed for the report. It is charming to read about the unexpected; such as the parties, being dive-bombed by skuas and the Russian hospitality that Karen experienced. It is clear to see that Karen was deeply moved by the reality for the Russians that took them to the other side of the world in order to make money for their families back home. There is nothing as enlightening as being on the edge of the world to make you appreciate the wonder and fragility of our planet and our fellow man.

As you turn the last page, you will understand why this book is called *The Impulsive Explorer*. From her spur of the moment decision to apply for the expedition to hanging up her corporate work shoes, Karen started to live life listening to her instincts. Her odyssey to the Antarctic was the catalyst which accelerated Karen's quest for freedom. You will no doubt resonate with her story and be encouraged to take a look at your life and perhaps be inspired to make different choices. Her JFDI message seems simple to me – you can be the creator of your own destiny and live a life on your terms.

Robert Swan, OBE, BA, FRGS – February 2021

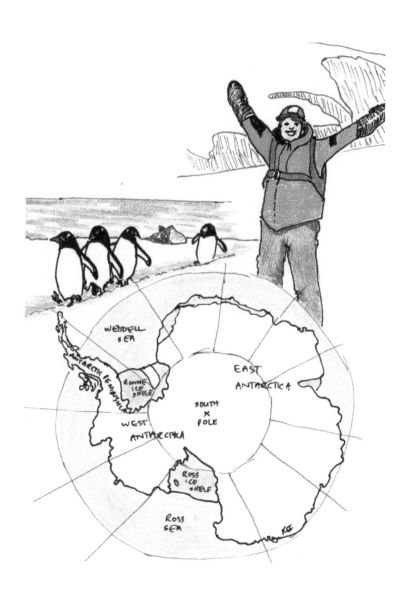

Introduction

'The real voyage of discovery consists not in seeking new landscapes, but in having new eyes.'
Marcel Proust, *Remembrance of Things Past*

L ike many thirty-somethings, reading *Bridget Jones' Diary* by Helen Fielding had struck a chord with me. Not least, the obsession for devouring self-help books in a pathetic attempt at finding the magic answer to 'IT' – love, wealth and happiness.

The obsession with self-help books slowly changed over time to 'downshifting' books as I searched for the secrets of becoming self-employed and fabulously wealthy with minimal effort (and finding the perfect partner as a convenient by-product!).

It started innocently enough with 'I could do anything I wanted if I only knew what it was,' but gathered momentum with countless books from *Who Moved My Cheese* to *Go It Alone*, *Your Money or Your Life*, *Successfully Going Freelance in a week* and so on ad nauseum. Through them, I was hoping to catch a glimpse of that other world, unfettered by what one colleague so aptly called 'Corporate Bollocks' – the politically back-stabbing, sabre rattling, gung-ho management world that seemed to be part and parcel of corporate life in the 80s and 90s.

My wildest fantasy of running a beach bar and windsurfing school somewhere hot and sunny beckoned enticingly, but friends who knew me better than I knew myself told me I would be bored witless within a season and besides which, what would I do in the winter? Not to be deterred, I investigated countries with year-round sunshine and finally found the ideal spot. Curaçao. No, not just a particularly noxious blue liqueur beloved of cocktail makers, but an island basking in 365 days of sun just off the north coast of South America. But the seeds of doubt had been sown and as with so many things in my life, this fell by the wayside, tripped up by my upbringing, and remains to this day a pipe dream.

Finally, however, in 2000, I took the plunge and what follows is the first part of my story about my attempts to free myself from the constraints of my family background and the golden handcuffs of full-time employment, to create a life lived on my terms and by my rules. It charts a trip that changed my life forever.

For those of you who are considering taking the same path, you may find some inspiration to help make that decision, or decide that life ain't so bad the way it is after all. But a word of warning: whilst your friends and family are right to be cautious and concerned on your behalf, 'there is danger in singing someone else's song' (Don G. Campbell) – it's your life and you only have one shot at it.

JFDI*

Chapter 1

Back to Before the Beginning

'Yet it is far better to light the candle than to curse the darkness.'
W.L. Watkinson, *The Invincible Strategy*

OK, so I've told you that I wanted to be master of my own destiny; how did it all start? It wasn't a sudden blinding flash of inspiration or a whim brought about by great unhappiness at work. The idea grew on me slowly. It was a bit like building a kit car. It gathered dust in my mental garage for years and every now and again, I would add a bit to it, grapple with the instructions, get overwhelmed with the enormity of the task, put it down in disgust, pick it back up again some time later, until eventually it was built. One day I was ready (and, more importantly, had the courage) to give the car one final flick of the duster, put the metaphorical key into the ignition, open the garage door and scream off down the leafy lanes to who knows where, throwing my trusty map out of the window as I went.

Rewind to the early 1960s. I was conceived in Nigeria where my father was working for a textiles company. Having been born in the UK, I then spent the first few months of my life back in Nigeria before being returned hurriedly along with my older brother to my grandparents when civil war broke out.

Until I was 18 and finally left home, our life was pretty transient as my father constantly moved us on to new countries. We were rarely anywhere for longer than three years and my formative years were spent variously in Northern Ireland, Malta and finally Hong Kong, with the UK thrown in between times for good measure. Hong Kong was where my father finally found his place – he loved it and luckily for me at the age of 13, I had stability at last and remained there until I was 18. Hong Kong was a fabulous place to grow up – certainly as the children of expats. My weekends were spent on the water; sailing, waterskiing, canoeing and windsurfing. There was no loitering about shopping precincts for us at weekends.

This was definitely my happy place. Being outdoors in great weather and doing physical activities I enjoyed, gave me a freedom to excel at doing things I loved without any obligations on the end results; unlike much of the rest of my life.

It's hard for me to describe my upbringing. On one hand, we had all our material needs catered for. We lived in nice houses and had lovely holidays – we were a typical middle-class family in that respect. On the other, it was a very strict childhood where discipline was generally physically administered.

Back in the 1950s and 60s, young people were expected to marry and have a family; my parents were no different. But for them, the job description only involved clothing, feeding and educating us. What they didn't feel a requirement was emotional support and love. Hugging was unheard of, and if we didn't do our chores on time or to the standard required, a spanking was called for. As children, we were very much to be seen and not heard. I was frightened of them because whatever you did, could so easily end up with a hand applied at speed, so you had to keep your wits about you. This could be for the smallest infringements, such as reading after lights out, or not cleaning your shoes (every day) on time.

I tried and tried to be the model daughter and do everything right. However, it was too easy to trip up and get it wrong.

When you don't have the option of standing your ground and you're constantly looking over your shoulder, worrying about when you'll next do something 'wrong', it leaves you fearful and helpless. You know that nothing you say will be heard. And when you are largely isolated from your friends, you don't get a perspective on what 'normal' looks like.

On the plus side, it started a lifelong love of reading. I would dive into books and the other worlds they opened up to me, allowing me to temporarily escape from my own reality.

Beyond that our parents said they didn't care what we did, as long as we were the best at it and academic qualifications the yardstick against which our success was measured. Of course, we were never quite good enough; we could always do better. It's a terrible burden to put on your children. Everything outside of getting a good education was surplus to requirements and extra curricular activities frowned upon as being a distraction to the main event and only allowed grudgingly and in small measures.

So, whilst my friends were all out partying and giving it large (although it wasn't called that in my day!) during their late teens, I would be found at home in my bedroom ostensibly studying. This wasn't so bad in the lower sixth form when I was allowed out until midnight on a Friday (and they knew to the minute how late I was, if I ever got home past the witching hour). By the upper sixth form, this privilege was removed and I had to be home by 9pm. As you can imagine, this was a source of great annoyance to my boyfriend who just could not understand why I didn't rebel and flout the rules. But he wasn't frightened of his parents and didn't have to live with their ire. I was operating on a cunning survival plan of getting out in one piece as fast as I could, and this meant getting to university.

I had to work particularly hard as I had been forced to take Chemistry A level when I really wanted to study art and go to art college. I wasn't the best art student, but I'd worked really hard for my O Level and something suddenly clicked and much to my surprise, I got an A. Painting is one thing I do (outside of reading) that I get totally absorbed by and can lose hours in happy distraction. And I love that a picture somehow magically grows from something that starts off as a terrible blob on the canvas. But art was not deemed to be a 'proper' subject and never going to make me any money, so Chemistry it was (so much for them not caring what we did as long as we were the best at it…). It never crossed my mind that I might have free will and be able (or allowed) to choose a life that wasn't one dictated by my parents. Any original thought that didn't align with theirs was dismissed as worthless. And I never found the courage to stand up to them. I have spent a lifetime trying to break free of that cage. My writing is part of that process.

I would have done far better in my other two subjects without the pain of trying to understand a subject which to this day remains shrouded in mystery. The actual exam was hideous. There was so much for me riding on getting the grades I needed that my mind went completely blank in one of the exams and I couldn't even draw a dot and cross diagram of an atom. I was sitting there sobbing quietly over my paper to the distress of my boyfriend who was sitting behind me – and who was one of those irritatingly brilliant people who didn't need to revise and still came out with three straight As! A teacher took pity on me and took me out and fed me tea. He was desperately trying to help me, but I wouldn't have any of it, being determined that I had to do it by myself or else feel a fraud.

Anyhow, I got through it and miraculously managed to get three Cs which was enough to get me my university place. I wanted to be a nurse having done some voluntary work at a hospital. Nursing appealed to my practical nature and a love of helping others. But my parents had much more grandiose ideas of me becoming a doctor. Bearing in mind that in those days you had to get As in Maths, Physics and Chemistry to get into medical school, I stood about as much chance of getting that as Bernard Manning did of becoming chairperson of Feminists International! So, we compromised. I would study to be a nurse, but also take a degree in Psychology at the same time in a combined degree course at St Bartholomew's Hospital and City University in London.

You cannot imagine my joy at the age of 18 as I skipped onto a train in Macclesfield with a trunk full of my worldly belongings and left home thinking I was free at last.

Of course, my parents didn't come with me to see me settled in to my new life in London. As they said to me as I left – we will pay your grant, but that's it, you're on your own, we've done our job now. But I didn't have one moment of homesickness and looked on in confusion as my fellow nurse students sobbed to their parents down the phone. In my head I was doing constant fist pumps of joy at my freedom.

Did I go a bit bonkers? You bet I did. I drank (a lot), I partied (a lot) and generally rolled around in the gloriousness of not having to answer to my parents. And luckily, they moved back to Hong Kong, so family visits were minimal.

I wasn't really free though – it's never that easy. The chains of your early life can be carried around for years. I didn't realise it, but everything I did was an attempt to gain my parents' love and approval, but it never seemed to be quite enough. Without that self-knowledge, I conducted my life with the flawed premise that one day I would be good enough for them to be proud of me, spurred on by their insistence that I could achieve the next promotion, have the big career and earn the huge salary. I did it all for their approval without wondering at the cost to myself.

I would like to add, as a bit of a counterbalance to the negative stuff, that my family life equipped me pretty well in other ways. My parents' insistence that we stand on our own two feet left me more than capable of leaving home at 18 and navigating my way through my early twenties. It made me fiercely independent (though rather bad at asking for help). And their emphasis on money being the root of all good, meant I was an excellent saver; I never borrowed more than I could pay back and had a fear of owing money. I was one of few people who left university without debt, having worked in pubs constantly to supplement my grant.

Having said that, fast forward to 1990 and you would have found me penniless, living in the granny annexe of a country pile near Salisbury, having recently separated from my husband of less than two years. My marriage was a classic example of me not listening to my instincts (which, on my wedding day, were to run very fast through the vestry and off into a different future). I married a man that my parents heartily approved of rather than someone who made my heart sing or really shared my vision for our long-term future. Needless to say, the cracks rapidly appeared and despite attempts to work through it, I found the courage to walk away from something that made me deeply unhappy.

It resulted in a long and dark 18 months during which everything I touched crumbled beneath my fingers, so much so that the man I was dating called me Unlucky Ed. I had been made homeless, changed jobs, moved cities, made redundant and lived on baked beans on toast in what had to be the coldest flat this side of the black stump (don't ask me where this is, just take it from me, it's a long way away!). My parents, ever supportive, basically told me to get a grip and not to complain as my unhappiness was entirely of my own making. They had not approved of me breaking up with my husband despite the fact that they hardly knew him with their move back to Hong Kong. In fact, they wrote to him apologising on my behalf! Nor had they approved of my career change. I was at rock bottom and I had my first bout of deep depression.

Luckily, I managed to get a new job at a health insurance company but I needed to buy a car to get to work and had no money to buy it. As my parents refused to help me out, I was very lucky that after a long search with my begging cap, one bank took pity on me and loaned me the money on the basis that I would get some money from my divorce to be able to pay it off. I have been with that bank ever since…thank you, Lloyds Bank! The divorce finally came through with a small sum of money that allowed me to get back on my feet and buy a small flat with a mortgage in Bournemouth.

Other than the fact that I knew that nothing could ever be that bleak again (or so I thought…) which was a valuable lesson, I also swore I would never be that poor again. Thus began many years of squirrelling money away into what fondly became known as my FOF (F**k Off Fund) against the day when I decided to throw it all in. Although, whether I would ever have the courage to do that was moot given my quest for parental approval which essentially meant getting promoted until I was Chief Executive of the universe, but even then, I should have my sights on taking over from God.

With life becoming more normal, and true to earlier form, I began the slow climb up the corporate ladder again. I was extremely lucky to have a boss who pushed me and pushed me until I finally broke after two years and agreed to start studying part-time for an MBA. It was clinched when I split up with my boyfriend and my boss said it was the perfect time as I'd have no distractions. What he neglected to tell me, was that I might as well have entered a convent for the next three years, as I wouldn't have time to date as well as work and study!

I shan't bore you with the next three years, but suffice it to say, it involved a lot of heartache, sweat and tears as I struggled to grapple with the intricacies of balance sheets and the mysteries of net present values. A positive side effect, as I'm sure those of you who have ever studied will recognise, is that my house was spotless. It was the equivalent of pencil sharpening as a diversionary tactic to avoid writing that essay on the globalisation of the ball bearing industry. I really **did** have to write an essay about those blasted ceramic balls; I didn't make that up!

I could not have survived it without the support of my fellow MBAers, who hauled me up from deepest depression and patiently handed me tissues to sob into on more occasions than I care to admit to. After what felt like three centuries, I finally emerged blinking back into the light again victoriously clutching my MBA certificate and was now a fully qualified Master of Bugger All as we affectionately called it. Of course, not content with this success, my parents wanted to know whether I had considered getting a further i.e. more respectable qualification from INSEAD or Cranfield. AAARRRRGGGGHHHH!

Despite all my whinging, I recommend an MBA if you have the stomach for it. My salary doubled from start to finish and not because my bosses suddenly saw my value, but entirely as a result of having more confidence in myself. Therefore, I applied for jobs that I would never have dreamed of being within my reach before. Amazingly enough, I always managed to blag my way into them. To this day I've had a fear that someone is going to tap me on the shoulder and say, 'OK, we've finally found you out for the fraud that you are. Now pack your desk up, put on this pinny and go and clean out the toilets'.

I know I'm not alone in this – I know of so many capable, intelligent women who struggle with Imposter Syndrome. Why do we do this to ourselves? It just holds us back whilst the men are busy trampling on our heads on the way to the top. Men seem to have this unwavering confidence in themselves which I have to say in some cases is very sadly misplaced; however, it seems to work. But let's not get into a debate on sexual politics in the workplace as I don't particularly want to get labelled so early on as a moustachioed, hairy arm-pitted, men bashing, carping feminist (although I am excellent at making sweeping generalisations!).

Where was I before I started down that slippery route? Oh yes, my giddy ascent up the career ladder, thanks largely to the confidence boosting qualities of an MBA and my upbringing. It (the MBA) just debunks so many myths (well, it did for me anyway) and gave me an understanding of words that previously might have well been in Russian for all that I understood their meaning. Now, I could bandy around words like globalisation, gearing and bi-polarised markets with gay abandon.

I owe a huge debt of gratitude to the encouragement and support I received from Norwich Union Healthcare who paid my fees and allowed me to use them as case studies (and not always flatteringly).

I moved to another health insurance company in my final year of studying at a much larger salary than the one I was on, thus adding extra funds to the slowly developing FOF.

It was a very surprising shock to go and work in an organisation in the 1990s and to discover that sexism was still alive and kicking, and whilst they were making great efforts to improve the situation, it was endemic. From the senior management down to the kitchen staff in the canteens, they were used to only men being in senior positions and I struggled for the brief time I was there to fit in. It was never overt or on a grand scale, it was much more insidious than that…

My boss at the time was the worst culprit. He'd make crass comments, like how it must have been my pretty smile that worked to get me into the car park at head office so easily (it was easier to get past Dobermans with elastic bands round their testicles than it was to get past the security guards there).

The canteen was an example from the other end of the spectrum. It operated on a card system whereby you had to credit your card with money before you could purchase anything. That is unless you were a Grade 7 manager or above, then you could hand over your card and the money would get deducted from your salary. I was the first female who had been employed at Grade 7. Having that seniority meant I was therefore entitled to the 'free' card. I went merrily in one day and got to the counter and the woman put my card in to the little machine, and told me that I had no money on the card and had to go and top it up. I looked blankly at her, she looked back at me puzzled and whispered, 'Are you a Grade 7 manager?' in awed tones whilst the thought bubble hovering over her head clearly said, 'That can't be right, you're female'. I don't know who was more embarrassed.

One of my male colleagues (who was actually a great ally) used to laugh about it and said that I had been called 'interesting and decorative' by some other senior managers. They really did not know how to deal with a 'gobby' female manager who knew her own mind.

It finally got to the stage where I had to sit my boss down and talk to him about it. It was a hilarious meeting. He'd obviously read the management books on how to talk to staff and duly pulled his chair round to sit on the same side of the desk as me, but then proceeded to cross both his arms and legs in a very defensive manner and twisted his body round so he was actually talking to the wall rather than me. And then on he rattled for the next 40 minutes or so about how the organisation used to be very male oriented but was changing and certainly none of his co-board appointed colleagues thought like that any more and so on ad infinitum. I sat there desperately trying not to giggle and thinking 'the man doth protest too much'. Eventually he finished and I gratefully escaped.

Yet within a week I had a call from one of his board appointed cronies informing me that he was coming down to visit our office in Bournemouth and wanted to meet with me to talk about something or other and we booked the time. Just as the conversation was drawing to a close, he asked to speak to the other manager who ran the centre. I told him he was out of the office that day and would in fact not be there when he came to visit. He said, 'Not to worry, but can you let someone else in a senior position know that I'm visiting?' Since I was the only other senior manager in the centre, I sweetly said to him, 'Well, I'm a Grade 7 manager too, will that be OK for you?' He blustered and laughed heartily before ringing off. I was livid and immediately wrote to my boss – I've never had a swifter reply, officially apologising.

The grading system in itself was eye-watering in its complexity. You started off at the bottom end of the scale as a Grade 1 and if you made it to management level, you got up to Grade 7. After that it became board-appointed management grades and there were another 5 or 6 of these disappearing off into the stratosphere.

I suspect it all changed when they merged with another insurance company. Dinosaur structures like this do not survive terribly well in this day and age, but I had left by the time the dust was settling on that. Before I left though, I had to re-apply for my own job despite being the only person who could actually do it as it was a very specialist role. Although, I had been responsible for writing the blurb that went out on the job sheets and by no great coincidence, it had been written in such a way that only a clone of me could possibly have replaced me internally.

Another classic example of Corporate Bollocks was the archaic furniture entitlement which depended entirely on your grading within the organisation. As a Grade 7 manager, I was entitled to an office, a desk with a return,

I was allowed to have a chair with arms (no one beneath this grade would dare ask for one of these!), a small sofa with coffee table, a bookshelf, a filing cabinet and the best of all… a wardrobe! Now other than being a great hiding place to escape from visiting board-appointed managers, I was never terribly clear about what I would need it for as I also had a coat stand!

I found the entrenched sexism very wearing – I've always felt that you should be rewarded on how good you are rather than whether you possess testicles… The final straw came one day when I was in personnel going over end of year bonuses for my staff. Unfortunately for the personnel administrator, she had a list of salaries on her screen. Unfortunate, because it listed my salary along with the rest of my management team (all men, remember) and I was being paid £4,000 less per annum than they were (this is the equivalent of approximately £8,000 today).

Luckily, 14 months into the job, I got headhunted and yet again, I managed to beat off the opposition and mysteriously landed myself another job. Conclusion: I must give good interviews! I've often wondered why this is. I can struggle to get an interview in the first place, but once I'm in, I stand a pretty good chance of getting the gig. I think it's probably due to the fact that I am so forthright and honest and am pretty much congenitally unable to bullsh*t and it must show. Though this has been a hindrance occasionally – it meant I was never put on gardening leave which was standard practice when

I moved from one insurance company to another. No lounging around in a garden on full pay waiting to start a new job for me. Damn me and my solid trustworthiness! I relocated from Bournemouth to Guildford for my next role with Standard Life Healthcare. I was very sad to move as I'd loved living in Bournemouth – I was close to the sea and all the outdoorsy stuff I loved being able to access so easily. But on, on up that career ladder I went.

In every job I'd had, I always claimed that I had never had to work as hard as I did in the latest job, and this was no exception. But for all that, it was very stimulating – I was setting up a new department and was able to build my own team and we were making a big difference to the business. My medical experience was really helpful and it was tremendous to have the freedom to create a department how I knew it should be run.

Thanks to that success, after two years I was asked to up the workload and take on a secondment to an IT project as the Business Manager whilst still continuing in my current position. We had been tasked with developing a brand-new system to run the business. Very exciting times! But talk about trying to juggle with 20 balls at the same time! There was so much to do and a lot of it for me in new territory. Inevitably, I started dropping a few, but somehow managed to pick them up and carry on albeit precariously. But it soon began to take its toll on me and I became a gibbering wreck. It would take very little for my lower lip to start wobbling and my desk, which was chaotic at the best of times, gradually took on epic proportions as paper piled ever higher and my to-do lists grew ever longer.

My behaviour must have been erratic and I can't have been a very pleasant work colleague. I was short tempered, I felt bullied being the only business manager amongst a team of IT boffins, and I often felt I was shouting into the wilderness. It culminated one day during a particularly heated meeting where I'd felt I'd been asked for one compromise too many. I drew myself up to my full five foot two inches, gathered up my mountains of files and stalked out desperately clinging on to the tatters of my dignity, only to collapse in floods of tears in the toilets (that haven of the distressed work female). At that moment I seriously doubted my ability to continue as I was in fear of my sanity.

But the Gods must have finally decided to smile on me and salvation lay on my chair when I arrived into work on the following Monday. Lying on my chair (as no one in their right minds left anything on my desk if they wanted me to see it) was a pale blue A4 sheet of paper entitled 'MISSION ANTARCTICA' in huge, glorious, bold type. Based as we were in Guildford, with the main insurance business up in Edinburgh, I had no idea that Standard Life had been sponsoring an environmental project to the Antarctic and that they were looking for participants for the third year.

With a sudden bolt of certainty, I knew I simply had to go. Scanning down the page, I discovered that there were two places available on a yacht sailing to the Antarctic as part of an environmental project with One Step Beyond (OSB). I skidded into Personnel quicker than a quick thing to get ahead of anyone else who might be applying (because I was sure that everyone would have read their flyer and felt as I did), snatched a form and went off clutching it to me as if my life depended upon it.

That night, I went home and filled in the form. There was only one major hitch as I could see it – my director had to approve the application. But as there was a very tight deadline on it, I had to see him as soon as possible and doing so was like trying to collect water with a sieve. But as soon as I could feasibly manage it, I snuck into his office.

The next half hour was difficult to say the least. The trip coincided with a critical stage of the project and quite frankly it was very inconvenient for the business. What was most upsetting though was the response. Firstly, he didn't think the trip was open to managers and therefore I wasn't eligible (wrong) and secondly, he didn't believe I deserved to go. He'd heard through the grapevine that I'd been looking for another job. Someone had misinterpreted my desperation and questioning as to whether I could physically and mentally continue as looking for another job.

Ah, the strong but unmistakable fishy whiff of Corporate Bollocks as I realised that someone had stitched me up like a kipper. He felt that only people who if you cut them in half had the company name running through them like a stick of Blackpool rock, deserved the opportunity. I had been that person twelve months ago, but apparently wasn't any longer. Well, you could have cut my legs off and called me even shorter. Gutted doesn't describe how awful I felt, that I thought he thought that little of me. Anyway, to be fair to him, he reluctantly agreed to complete the form, safe in the knowledge that there was no way I would get chosen. I crept out of his office a broken woman, my self-confidence already shaky, now in little pieces around my ankles.

I can, in retrospect, see his point. The last thing he needed was for me to go, particularly if he thought I was going to jump ship in any case. But he could so easily have turned it round saying he could see I was de-motivated and perhaps a trip to the Antarctic could be the very thing to get me back to my previous level of enthusiasm. But why use a carrot when a stick will do?

I almost resigned there and then, but I wanted to go to the Antarctic so badly it hurt, and I was prepared to swallow my pride for that. What a different tale to tell had I resigned at that point. I would never have gone south and this book would be missing a whole chapter. No, in fact, this book probably would never have been written as I more than likely would have found another job and still be chained to a desk as I write. There, I've given it away, suspense over – I got to go to the Antarctic. But not without a few more hurdles.

JFDI

Chapter 2

The Quest for Antarctica

'He who dares, wins.'
Del Boy Trotter, *Only Fools and Horses*

Within two days of my application being sent off, I had a phone call, last thing on Friday afternoon. Could I please produce a five-minute video giving the reasons why I should be chosen, the benefits to the company and to myself? Oh, and could it please be with us by first thing Wednesday morning?

Do what???

I had never used a video camera before in my life, let alone produced a slick promo of myself. Where to find a video camera at short notice? I discovered that you cannot rent cameras for love nor money (at least not in Guildford in 1999).

The next question was – what on earth could I do? I really didn't want to sit looking idiotically into a camera dully and earnestly telling them why I should go. So, it had to be eye-catching and amusing, whilst at the same time getting an important message across. A mad idea of hitching my cat up to sledge traces whilst pretending to 'mush' her across snowy plains was quickly discarded on the grounds that a) there were no snowy plains easily to hand, b) it was too flippant and most pertinently, c) she's a cat and therefore I had two hopes of catching her, let alone training her.

Then, Eureka! I had it! I'll interview myself, I thought. Me in posh suit interviewing me in ski gear. All I had to do was write the script, find a video camera (learn how to work video camera), get props, film self, edit film and send it off, all by first post on Tuesday!

Have you ever tried talking to a camera whilst smiling at the same time? My respect for television presenters went up in leaps and bounds as I endlessly re-shot myself, trying to arrange my features into something other than that of a very grim gargoyle. If bad news had to be delivered to the nation, I'd be the very fellow for the job – I'd have them on their knees prostrate with grief with my expression alone.

However, I finally partially succeeded after umpteen 'takes' and eventually managed to get the film in the can, as we in the movie business like to say, having spent a further very frustrating two hours trying to edit out my leaping up to switch the video on and off in between costume changes.

Astoundingly, it did the trick and I found myself flying up to Edinburgh for the final assessment along with five other hopefuls (much to the distress of my boss, who was now convinced I was going to get a place).

The day went dreadfully for me, not helped by a particularly nasty dose of PMT. We were required to do lots of team games to see how we worked together solving 'real life' situations. It was a strange environment where we were all being desperately nice to each other to prove that we could work in a team whilst simultaneously trying to eliminate the opposition.

I really had no energy for it. Trying to compete with others, who seemed to be leading quite well enough without my input, just didn't seem right. I think my saving grace was my presentation where I dreamed up a 7 'C' model of customer care (thank you once again, MBA) complete with badly drawn cartoons to illustrate the dangers of ignoring customers.

I departed in the evening feeling completely emotionally drained after a day that ended with a particularly gruelling interview resigned to not going after all.

We'd been told we would know by the following Tuesday and when the phone call finally came through, I was a bag of nerves. It was too early, they were clearly telling the unfortunate ones first before giving the good news to the successful two. I was told to sit down. 'Here goes,'

I thought, the gentle rejection, great candidate and all that, but unfortunately others were better; you get the picture. So, when I was offered the place, I was absolutely gobsmacked and disbelieving. But as the realisation dawned that I was actually going, I could feel a huge bubble of excitement rising up in me and it exploded as I leapt to my feet thumping the air with a victory fist pump.

'I WAS GOING TO THE ANTARCTIC!!!' I shouted in my head.

On hanging up, my colleague asked me, 'Good news?' I shrugged my shoulders nonchalantly as I tried to put a lid on my euphoria, realising my boss really ought to be the first to hear. I walked up to the fourth floor, grinning like a Cheshire cat and I didn't need to tell him, he could see for himself. In true restrained style, he solemnly shook my hand, unlike the MD who gave me a big kiss! I couldn't wait to tell my parents who were coming down to stay for a few days. I rushed home and told them I had some really exciting news.

The response? You should be able to guess by now. 'You've been made director', they chorused excitedly. Once they'd got over that disappointment though, they managed to turn it around in their heads and said how good that was going to look on my CV. At this point, a little realisation started to dawn on me – that I was never going to get to a point where I was going to fulfil their wildest dreams for me.

I still had another six months to wait before I went and the number of times I almost resigned in the meantime doesn't bear thinking about. It was only the thought of the Antarctic that sustained me through the worst excesses of the continually delayed project from hell and the bollockings that went with it.

The expedition had originally been going to sail across the Drake Passage in an ex 'Round The World Race' yacht. It's an infamous stretch of water in the southern oceans from Cape Horn down to the Antarctic Peninsula where the Atlantic meets the Pacific. It has notoriously rough seas and storms that strike fear into the heart of even the sturdiest sailor.

Whilst I had done a lot of dinghy sailing and some big yacht stuff in the past, I'd never been out of sight of land and I was a tad nervous about how I would cope in big seas. I thought I'd better have a trial run to see what I had let myself in for. I'd gone to a boat show with a friend and decided to sign up (and pay) to be part of a crew on a cross channel yacht race from Southampton to Cherbourg.

It all started well. We sailed out into the Sound in the early evening and headed for the eastern headland of the Isle of Wight. There was a good wind and the seas were calm. But as we came around the headland and headed for open waters, the winds picked up and the seas got choppier and rougher. I'd only chosen the night for gale force winds of between 8 and 9 on the Beaufort Scale. This is pretty bloody windy! Perfect practice for the Drake Passage. The yacht rolled about alarmingly and even as I sat with my legs over the side and tried to watch the horizon, I started to feel increasingly queasy. I thought lying down might help but all I could then see was the mast doing crazy rotating things, which really didn't help so I rapidly sat up again. I started hallucinating at one stage where buoys turned into great big chequered castles. And then, to top it all, I began to heave over the side of the yacht before the skipper suggested I should probably go and lie down in the cabin. I was marginally mollified by seeing one of the other members of the crew also hanging over the side and he was a RNLI volunteer!

Because it was a racing yacht, the berths consisted of aluminium frames with netting across them (who has time to sleep during a race is the logic, I guess). They plonked me into a berth, handed me a bucket and winched me in so I couldn't roll out and then left me to it.

I spent the next 10 hours in complete misery. Seasickness is unremitting in its awfulness and I vomited on and off for the whole time. Even when I had nothing left to give, my body spasmed and tried to eject my stomach. I remember being desperate to use the heads (on-board loo), but every time I moved a muscle it set off another spasm and I felt I was going to be trapped in that hell for life.

A seasoned sailor once told me that new sailors at sea spend the first day being terrified that they are going to die, but when the seasickness takes hold, they then spend the next day hoping they will do! This is exactly how I felt.

I only started feeling better as daylight approached and we hit the calmer waters of Cherbourg. On the plus side, the nausea faded pretty quickly once the boat steadied. I staggered up on deck looking like death, revelling in the fact I was going to survive, but feeling rather awful that I hadn't been of any help in the race whatsoever. I had effectively paid a sum of money to purge myself!

The return trip was, thankfully, better. Even though there was a big swell after the storm, it was daylight and they sensibly put me on the helm to steer the ship that enabled me to concentrate on the horizon.

This experience really didn't bode well for my passage to the Antarctic. But at the same time, I wanted to be one of the few people who could say they had sailed across the Drake Passage. Five days of seasickness in each direction would be a small price to pay for that honour.

But then, disaster (or given my experience, a happy accident!) struck. The yacht, *2041*, wasn't going to get to Ushuaia in time for our arrival – teething problems after its refit. I was bitterly disappointed convinced that Unlucky Ed had made an appearance again. I struggled for weeks to convince myself it was still going to be an amazing trip – how ungrateful could a girl get? As it turned out, the trip was very different from previous expeditions and to my mind far better. But, I'm getting ahead of myself.

You might be asking yourself at this point, what was a large corporate organisation doing sending people to the Antarctic on an environmental project?

As I mentioned earlier, the trip was organised through One Step Beyond, an organisation set up by Robert Swan. What to say about him other than he is the first person to have walked to both poles, which is a pretty amazing accomplishment in itself. He was first inspired by the story of Captain Scott and his dream became to follow 'In the footsteps of Scott' (which also became the title of his book and is well worth a read, if for no other reason than to see how people with very different personalities get along under extreme circumstances). Back in 1979, he set about raising the £2.5 million needed to get a team of five to the South Pole. Fundraising seems to be the most difficult aspect of any expedition and is a recurring theme of any expeditioner/explorer you read about. Once the money has been raised, the rest is apparently easy!

Having finally raised the funds, he along with two colleagues, Roger Mear and Gareth Wood, left behind the rest of the team having overwintered in the Antarctic and set off on the 900-mile trek across the Polar ice cap. Eventually, on 11th January 1986, they arrived at the South Pole. The arrival couldn't have been more different from Scott's. They were greeted by the Americans who have a base there, so none of the awful disappointment of Scott who not only had to swallow the bitter pill that Amundsen had reached the Pole before him, but then had to face the perilous, and ultimately fatal, return journey.

However, they had their own disaster when their ship, the Southern Quest, was crushed by the ice pack on the way to the Antarctic to deliver a plane to take the team away, leaving the crew stranded on the ice after the ship sank.

Fortunately, everyone was removed safely and there were no casualties, but not without a huge amount of fuss raised by the Americans who were dead set against what they considered maverick and unqualified amateurs deciding to have a 'jolly' down in the Antarctic. It is testament to Robert that he managed, at great financial loss to himself, to return the expedition back to civilisation whilst ensuring they cleared out all the rubbish they had generated in being there.

The experiences left him fired with an environmental zeal and he was determined to tell the world about the environmental problems we continue to create for ourselves.

Robert was given a 50-year mission by famed oceanographer Jacques Cousteau to protect the polar region back in 1991 and set up the 2041 Foundation as a result. The mission of the 2041 Foundation is to engage businesses and communities on climate science, personal leadership, and the promotion of sustainable practices, and to try and ensure that the Antarctic Treaty gets renegotiated.

The Antarctic Treaty covers the protection of the Antarctic as a sanctuary for science and peace. It is up for renegotiation in 2048 and there will be a great deal of pressure to open it up to mining companies, which will be an ecological disaster.

Through the foundation, Robert uses his great personal commitment and drive as a motivational speaker, talking to anyone who will listen about his adventures, using them as a platform to raise corporate awareness about the damage we are doing to the planet. His charitable organisation, OSB, was set up to carry out environmental projects and to use as many people from different nations as possible in the hope that if enough people know and talk about the issues, then things might change.

It was his talk to Standard Life that fired them with an enthusiasm for what he does and they agreed to sponsor OSB for four years on the condition that two members of staff would go to the Antarctic for each year of the sponsorship. The particular expedition was Mission

Antarctica – a project aimed at removing all the waste at a Russian base, Bellingshausen, on King George Island off the Antarctic Peninsula.

JFDI

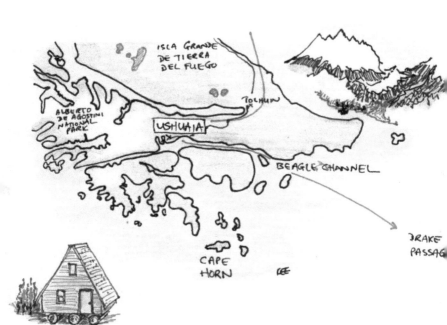

Chapter 3

On Our Way

'You're off to Great Places! Today is your day! Your mountain is waiting, So… get on your way!'
Dr Seuss, *Oh, The Places You'll Go!*

I was manically busy on the work project whilst at the same time preparing for my trip to the Antarctic. This included various briefings, talking to previous expeditioners, understanding what was expected of us on our return and buying a mountain of kit suitable for life in the freezer – fleeces, walking boots, coats, rucksacks, waterproof bags, gloves, trousers, hats, and on and on. Thanks to the generosity of Standard Life, everything was paid for – I was out of pocket for nothing and 20 years later, I still have a lot of the clothing!

I also needed to leave a mass of instructions for those left behind on what needed to be done on the project to make sure things stayed on track whilst I was away.

Finally, the 21st January 2000 arrived, and I was ready to go.

You'd think I was going for six months and not six weeks with the mountain of kit I had – a huge sailing bag, video equipment, water collection box (for some research I was going to do) and a day sack. In my panic to get to the airport on time, I arrived far too early and then started worrying as to whether I was at the right place and had to keep checking my ticket to make sure. This was a classic symptom of the frightened flier (i.e. me) along with the recurring nightmares of being at the wrong airport, passport left at home or luggage been lost en route.

Bronco, our expedition leader, and Richard, the cameraman, had left a few days ahead of us to make advance preparations, so the only other person I knew was Alison, my co-partner from Standard Life, who was late and I had no idea who I was looking for.

I must just divert slightly here and talk about Bronco. He came to meet me a few weeks before our departure to brief me on the plans for the trip. Now, if someone said to you, your expedition leader is Bronco Lane, what image would you conjure up? My particular image was of a six foot five blonde American hunk. The name just screams beefcake, doesn't it? You can picture my face then, when a fifty-something, medium-height man appeared in reception. I also noticed that he had no fingers on one hand and over lunch I discovered that he also had no toes. My first thoughts were, this man is taking us camping on a glacier and he's digitally challenged, how careless can a man get? I am so embarrassed now that I could have even entertained such thoughts but it just goes to show how wrong first impressions can be. Bronco is nothing short of a hero and as far as I am concerned, he walks on water.

This mild-looking man was in the SAS, has climbed Everest on several occasions, reaching the summit once, and it was during this trip that he and his 'oppo', Brummie Stokes, got caught in the mother of all storms on their descent, resulting in major frostbite. What is actually amazing is that he only lost a few fingers and toes. And the tales he told us would make your toes curl (but not his obviously!). As a man who firmly believes in the Official Secrets Act, I can't begin to imagine what he **didn't** tell us and all told in a completely understated matter of fact manner as if he had done nothing more extraordinary than go to Sainsbury's to do the weekly shop. He has been a source of great inspiration to me and a stout supporter of my endeavours since I met him, so Bronco, I owe you a huge apology for getting it so wrong back then.

Back to the airport, and eventually the others started drifting in. My naïve hopes of forging a tight knit team started to unravel as I realised that some of them had already checked themselves in. I thought we'd all be checking in together and sitting next to each other on the plane, but no. I was a little surprised and not a little disappointed. What added to my chagrin was that I got lumped with a huge excess luggage charge with the video equipment and research stuff which, had we all checked in at once, we could have redistributed and avoided the charge. I was only faintly mollified when the slightly dippy attendant at the check-in desk got confused by my Mission Antarctica labels, thought we were missionaries and hence reduced my charges. Perhaps she thought we were off to preach the gospel to penguins or something! Who was I to disabuse her, so muttering, 'God bless you,' under my breath, I scuttled off to pay the fine before she realised her error.

The flight to Buenos Aires was uneventful and we transferred to the internal airport to catch our flight down to Ushuaia in Tierra del Fuego (the pointy bit at the bottom of South America). There was a slight panic as our lady on the scene realised she'd left our tickets on the dressing table at home (which proves that my nightmares are not totally without substantiation!), but as we had plenty of time there was no need to worry unduly. She left behind her six rather bewildered and brain-dead strangers staring at each other over their luggage trolleys.

And what an eclectic bunch of people we were! I don't think I could have put together a more diverse set of people if I'd tried. There was Chris, the head teacher from Cumbria, who looked like some latter day explorer in his lumberjack shirt and huge bushy beard; Nattapong ('Nat' for short), a 21-year-old from Thailand – so polite and quiet that you never really knew what he was thinking;

Alex, the 25-year-old eco warrior and blonde goddess who drove Zodiacs (inflatable dinghies with an outboard motor) for Greenpeace and volunteered for the RNLI; Siaron, a triathlete from Royal and Sun Alliance; and Alison, a petite, dark-haired Irish dynamo from Standard Life, who like Siaron was an experienced walker; and, then there was little old me! Reading through their bios, I was struck with the amount of experience they had between them and felt like the cuckoo in the nest and totally inadequately prepared for what lay ahead.

As we had a few hours to kill after we checked in, we wandered over the road to sit by the River Plate to enjoy the sun after the miserable weather in the UK. It felt really bizarre being there as everyone spoke Spanish and it certainly didn't feel like we'd crossed to another continent at all. The Plate is an enormous river; it looked more like the sea and you could not see the other shore. It was also filthy.

There were islands of plastic bottles floating against the pier, but it didn't stop the locals from fishing (using chorizo as bait!). Not that we ever saw them catch anything: 'Hey, honey, you'll never believe the whopper I caught today – it was a 22lb coke bottle, it'll look great mounted on the wall!'

Finally, after burning ourselves to a crisp and sweating profusely in our jeans and fleeces, we boarded our plane and headed south to Ushuaia. Our excitement mounted as we flew over the mountains covered in snow and the lakes twinkling like emeralds in the sunlight. And then there was Ushuaia, a tiny town clinging to the coast at the head of the Beagle Channel!

Bronco and Richard were waiting for us as we cleared customs, Bronco beaming and Richard hiding behind his camera as he filmed our arrival. He was a real surprise too. A wizened little man who as far as we could tell existed solely on a diet of nicotine and gin, and goodness knows what would happen to him if he gave up either. He had a tongue on him that could lacerate at 100 paces. There was nothing he didn't have a strong and intractable opinion on and woe betide you if you got on the wrong side of him. But he was an excellent raconteur and cameraman, even if he did on occasion forget that he'd already told you a story several times before – it was best not to tell him. He decided to adopt me and he became my film mentor and smoking partner. My vain idea of giving up smoking had failed after I received an email from him telling me that cigarettes were less than 50 pence a packet and I'd be mad not to. With the breaking strain of a wet KitKat, I crumbled and many happy hours were spent railing against the world whilst smoking (and drinking gin in his case), hidden away in his cabin.

We spent two days in Ushuaia making the final preparations and getting to know each other. Richard gave us lessons in film-making, Bronco briefed us on the next stage of the trip, I interviewed everyone on film and we bought brew kit for our stay on Bellingshausen plus gifts for our soon-to-be Russian hosts. A nice simple task, you'd think, to buy shampoo, toothpaste and combs for 25 people. The shampoo and toothpaste were simple enough, but trying to find 25 identical combs in Ushuaia, the town that time forgot, proved to be slightly trickier. We scoured the main shopping centre for hours before finally emerging, tired but victorious, clutching our trophies to us.

Mind you, it doesn't take that long to 'do' Ushuaia. It is essentially one very long road with a mixture of tourist shops full of the usual highly inflated tourist tat purchased with great enthusiasm by the predominantly ageing American cruising population, along with the everyday shops for the locals. Outside of this main drag is the 'smart' residential area – houses made of bricks and mortar at least. But then very quickly they give way to odd little triangular wooden houses built on logs and painted in all colours of the rainbow. There used to be a law that prohibited anyone living on the same bit of land for more than five years. So, with great cunning and adaptability, they built their houses on logs and once every five years, they would simply roll them to a new location. It adds a whole new meaning to moving house!

Its only claim to fame is that it is the southernmost city in the world and it played on it shamelessly. Let's face it, there's not a lot else to Ushuaia. T-shirts emblazoned with 'El Fin del Mundo' (the end of the world) were the fashion *du jour.* It was originally established as a prison colony, but the prison is now a museum, home to dusty relics of a bygone era along with tales of Antarctic expeditions. Not the most riveting of tourist attractions, but the best Ushuaia had to offer.

At last, departure day arrived and we bundled our kit onto the minibus and headed for the port and onto the *Sergey Vavilov* – an ex-Russian research vessel converted into a small cruise ship. We were very tickled to learn that the captain was named Kalashnikov.

Having stored our kit into our compact cabins, we had a couple of hours to kill so I took the opportunity to send a quick email. Back in 2000, the internet was still a relatively new thing and I loved it! It didn't matter where you were in the world, there always seemed to be an internet cafe somewhere, allowing you to keep in touch. I dashed off a quick report before returning excitedly to the ship. It's so exciting leaving on a cruise ship, you feel like royalty as everyone onshore waves you off, running alongside the quay.

The departure down the Beagle Channel was beautiful. It was early evening and there wasn't a breath of wind – it was like sailing on silver silk as the water rippled away from us, glistening in the setting sunset. It was just our ship and the hills soaring up on either side with a few birds settling down for the night. Having investigated the ship, from the bridge to the library and eaten a delicious dinner, we clambered into our berths. With my tendency to seasickness, I wasn't taking any chances, so I took my travel sickness tablets and strapped on my sea-bands, ready to face the slings and arrows of the Drake Passage early the next morning.

Then, just as I thought that nothing could stop us, Unlucky Ed struck again. I'll leave it to Richard's report to describe the event as he tells it far better than I could:

28 Jan 2000, Report from Richard Wade, on-board *Vavilov*

'Our cabin is on the port side and, as I look out of the porthole, I have a beautiful view of Cape Horn, which is strange as it should be on the other side of the boat. When we were steaming down the Beagle Channel last night, the ship was doing a good 20 knots. Now we are just making steerage way at about three knots, if that. The ship has two 3500 HP engines which run at a constant speed and turn two variable pitch propellers which are computer driven to provide infinitely variable speed both ahead and astern. The computer's motherboard has fried during the night and however fast the propellers turn, the blades remain almost flat. Which is better than the hour and a half during the small hours when we were going backwards at eight knots. So the emergency system is now in operation and they have been able to adjust the blades manually so that we are not completely helpless. The bow and stern thrusters have also stopped working. It is a system designed and built b `⋅` *the Swiss, who, as most people are aware, are famous*

making cuckoo clocks. Their understanding of the seas has, to my knowledge, always been limited. It also seems that the instruction book says that only their engineers can repair the system and they, of course, are at this moment tucking into a large bowl of fondue in Geneva. I think, perhaps, we are about to spoil their day.

So, tugs have been called and the pilot will be back aboard at noon. We must look on the bright side. There is no shipwreck and nobody drowned – it might be much worse. The sea is like a mill pond and the sky is blue. We might now easily be in a force nine in the middle of the Drake Passage with little chance of keeping the ship's head into wind. We might easily be surrounded by icebergs bearing down on us. We might have run out of whisky. As it is we shall be back in Ushuaia in about fifteen hours and the yacht club pours a mean gin and tonic.'

It was with very heavy hearts and a feeling of impending doom that we returned alongside the dock at Ushuaia.

Our time was not completely wasted, as we took the opportunity to clamber the steep path up to the glacier and take in the views of the Beagle Channel from a great height. The rest of the time was spent in briefings with Jonas, the ship's tour master, who called us in for meetings to advise us on the latest news as to the progress of our as yet elusive new motherboard. One calamity built on another as we discovered that no one really knew where the engineer was or when he was actually going to arrive. He was finally tracked down to Florida where he promptly got grounded by a hurricane and it was all very touch and go as to whether he was going to get to us by the Sunday which was our D-Day. If he didn't arrive then AND fix the ship, that was it, the trip was cancelled.

Thus began our desperate search for another berth. Unfortunately, all the big cruise liners were fully booked, there were no yachts heading our way and the *Oosterschelde*, a beautiful four-masted barque, was not leaving for a while yet (although Alison and I were hatching desperate plans to hijack it). The only alternative was a rowing boat that I spotted outside the Yacht Club, but whilst Shackleton may have been able to navigate himself across the Antarctic oceans, I didn't hold out much hope for us. My sense of direction not being great at the best of times.

In the meantime, life aboard the ship was beginning to grate on my nerves.

Whilst we had been scaling the glacier, I had despatched Richard, who had declined to join us (as climbing even a slight ascent would more than likely have been the death of him!) on a mission to buy me some parcel tape. He signally failed, but we spotted some behind the bar on-board and smuggled it out under his fleece. Thus began, Operation Tannoy Muffle…

For those of you who have been on cruises before, maybe you are familiar with regular Tannoy messages. For the rest of you, it would appear that by boarding a cruise ship, your short to medium term memory is left dockside. This means that although a printed itinerary of the next day's activities is slipped unobtrusively under the door of your cabin each night, you will be rendered completely incapable of remembering:

a.   what the activities are
b.   what time they start, or
c.   where they take place

Luckily for us, the tour staff had realised this mental problem existed and solved it by ensuring that messages about forthcoming activities were blasted into all cabins starting at 7.15am with an unnecessarily bright and breezy 'Hi De Hi Campers!' heartiness that only Americans seem capable of. 'Good morning, ladies and gentlemen, breakfast will be served at 7.30 until 8.15 this morning. This will then be followed by a talk in the lecture room by Rick on the mating habits of benthic plankton in the Antarctic Convergence zone in the latter weeks of March.'

You may be forgiven for thinking that at this point you would be able to roll over and catch a few more zeds – not a bit of it. At 7.45 we were reminded again about the 8.30 talk and because you are incapable of holding a thought for more than five minutes, you would then get a further call at 8.25 that it is in the lecture room on Deck 6. Thank goodness they reminded us of its location even though there was only one lecture room and strange as it may seem, it remained on Deck 6 for the duration of the journey!

Needless to say, this drove me quietly (and more dangerously, homicidally) demented. Hence the implementation of Operation Tannoy Muffle. A bright blue and yellow pillow kindly donated by Richard was taped inelegantly and inexpertly to the speaker in the cabin (with the purloined parcel tape). Siaron was so impressed with my handiwork, that at 1.30 in the morning we attached towels to hers. It helped, marginally, but not as successfully as I would have hoped, but combined with ear plugs it allowed me to lie in the following morning until 8.45 before the dulcet tones of Monica finally penetrated the fog of sleep.

All this helped to distract us slightly from the worries of the potential on-going non-going status of the trip. My diary at the time was full of great rantings against the unfairness of it all as I struggled with the concept of que sera sera.

Finally, Sunday afternoon arrived, and in our nervousness, we left the ship until we thought the engineer may have boarded. Further delays as the engineer missed his plane and finally appeared in the early evening. We spent an hour marching restlessly like expectant fathers in the lobby of the ship along with some last-minute travellers who were hoping to hitch a ride. In an attempt to distract and entertain people, I walked on my hands which caused great cheering. Unfortunately, it had the effect of making other passengers think the ship had been fixed and they came dashing down the corridors to see what the fuss was about.

…Only me!

Anyway, joy of joys and despite my deep cynicism that a change of motherboard would do the trick, the engineer worked miracles with the props and at last we were on our way again. What excitement as we set off for the second time down the Beagle Channel. Then horror of horrors, we slowed, stopped and started reversing! I'll never forget Alison's face as she ran towards me along the rail with alarm writ large upon her! Luckily, it was just a test and soon we were under full steam again! This time, we were really going.

JFDI

Plastic bottles on the River Plate

At the supermarket with Nat buying combs and toothpaste for the Russian base

The Vavilov docked in Ushuaia – our transport across the Drake Passage

Beautiful calm evening as we departed for Cape Horn down the Beagle Channel

The Oosterschelde – the yacht we were planning on hijacking!

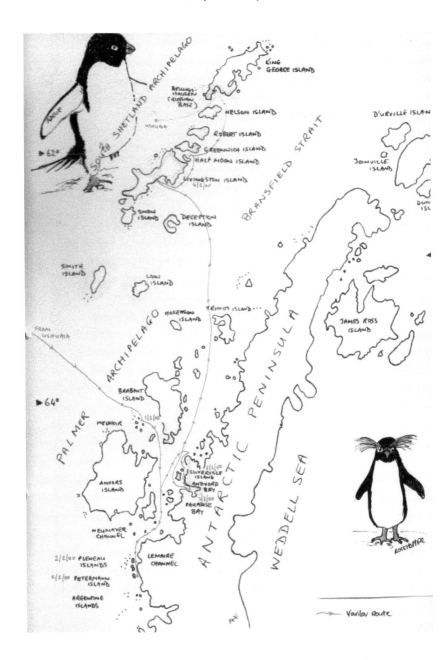

Chapter 4

Icebergs and Russian Vodka

'Antarctica left a restless longing in my heart beckoning towards an incomprehensible perfection forever beyond the reach of mortal man. Its overwhelming beauty touches one so deeply it is like a wound.'
Edwin Mickleburgh, Be*yond the Frozen Sea*

The journey across the Drake Passage was uneventful, yet very exciting for Alison. Her enthusiasm was very refreshing for those of us with slightly more jaded temperaments. It was, however, less exciting for Chris and Nat who were both grossly unwell and disappeared completely for two days as they lay prostrate in their cabin together. The sea wasn't particularly rough – at least not for the Drake – but there was a huge swell which hit the boat side on and it rolled around alarmingly and rather nauseatingly.

Mealtimes were quite interesting and involved a lot of sliding plates and cups. You soon learnt how to time the picking up of glasses full of liquid. The chairs were attached to the floor by chains which gives you some indication of how rough it can get. I found it all a bit sick-making but survived pretty well until one night I was trying to ignore the nausea and was testing some of the passengers with lateral thinking quizzes. I ignored it too long, when suddenly I had to excuse myself and accelerated rapidly down the corridor to the heads and only just made it in time. Unfortunately, I ended up decorating the walls of the toilet more than actually hitting the target. Just what I needed, to have to clear up the mess whilst feeling like death warmed up. Seasickness, as I described earlier, is absolutely foul. There is nothing you can do to make yourself feel better and the best thing to do is just lie down and hope that you hit terra firma soon (the firma the ground, the lesser the terra!).

Our fellow passengers were a very eclectic mix. The majority were retired elderly Americans busy spending their old age and pensions seeing the world that they never had time to when they were younger. At first, I was a little unsure about them, thinking that they were quite the wrong sort of people to be visiting the Antarctic. Just not PLU, darlings (People Like Us – hardened explorers that we were!). I assumed they would be unimpressed by what we were going to see and more interested in taking snaps of 'lil' ol' Andardica'. But whilst some of them did find it quite difficult getting in and out of Zodiacs and skidded around rather dangerously on the ice, my opinion quickly changed once I started talking to them. They were easily as awestruck as we were.

Although I am pleased to say that my stereotyping wasn't without some justification when it came to mealtimes. There were mountains of food on-board and it was superb; buffets and five-course dinners were standard (assuming you had any appetite to eat which I didn't for the two-day passage crossing). But the minute the food gong was announced, you'd think we were about to face our last meals as they barged their way into the dining room and piled their plates with all the goodies on offer.

There was also a small contingent of younger travellers who were just wandering around the world, and some of their stories were amazing and made me realise how narrowly I'd lived my life.

And then there were the twitchers! Easily identifiable in their camouflage kit (on a 5-star cruise ship, I ask you!), muffled up to the eyebrows in balaclavas, draped about with cameras, tripods and binoculars. They maintained a constant, if somewhat sinister looking, vigil on the upper decks and bridge at all hours of the day. Thanks to them, they told us of all the bird life that was fluttering around. Not that I ever got to grips with the differences between a tern and a storm petrel!

The crew were fantastic. The bulk of the crew were Russians (it being a Russian ship, I don't suppose that should have been a surprise, but it was). They were extremely friendly, even if we couldn't communicate terribly well with them. I tried to practice my Russian on them in an attempt to be able to at least say hello in Russian once we arrived at our final destination. They were very kind to me, and smiled encouragingly, but I could tell from their blank stares that I really wasn't making any sense at all. I managed to finally get to grips with 'please,' 'thank you,' and 'you're welcome,' but not much more than that.

The remainder of the crew were European and American. The head chef, Helmut, was another character, an eccentric Austrian who spent his summers visiting really out of the way places, and who entertained us endlessly with his stories. He once subjected us to an evening of Tyrolean dancing, fully clad in thigh-slapping lederhosen which caused almost too much excitement with some of our more elderly passengers!

After two very long nights and days, an iceberg was spotted – the Antarctic was finally in sight. And we aren't talking little floating blocks of ice, we are talking huge great whopping mountains of ice. The ice in the Antarctic is absolutely amazing, the colours are beyond description – glistening whites and translucent blues, and shapes which would have had Salvador Dali rushing for his paint box.

We anchored for the night in a bay and before it became dark, they launched the Zodiacs and took us on a mini tour of the bay. It was fantastic just cruising along the coast seeing a few sea lions and our first sightings of penguins. Then our driver cut the engine and we drifted silently on the sea... except it wasn't silent. You could hear a fizzing noise, like the noise you hear when you put your ear to an open can of Coke. It was the ice melting and releasing trapped air into the sea. What is even more staggering is that the air was over 2,000 years old, trapped when the ice was first formed! From that point onwards, all our ship-side drinks were cooled with lumps of this ice – pretty amazing, eh? Beats any novelty heart shaped ice cubes hands down.

We continued motoring during the night and for once I didn't mind the tannoy which woke us at 5.30, for we had arrived at the Lemaire Channel, or Kodak Alley as it is otherwise known due to its outstanding photogenic qualities. We were blessed for once with glorious sunshine (as it was summer down there, there were still only a few hours of darkness during a 24-hour period) and the sight took our breath away. Huge towering mountains on either side that completely dwarfed the ship, covered in vast glaciers pushing their way down to the sea with the peaks covered in fluffy white and pink clouds. It's so hard to describe the views and do them justice and I simply can't – I had to let the photographs and video do the talking on my return. It was so peaceful standing on the deck supping our hot chocolate and vodka (well, it was on offer and free – and it seemed churlish to refuse) with just the quiet hum of the engines surrounded by this epic panorama of nature at its best.

Sadly, it was over too soon and we headed off to the Melchior Islands for an iceberg tour. If possible, this was even more amazing (sorry, but there's a lot of usage of the word 'amazing' – I ran out of superlatives very early on in the trip). Once again, they unloaded the Zodiacs and with six of us to a boat, we motored into an iceberg field. For two hours we just cruised around surrounded by these monoliths filled with little tunnels of ice and beautiful shapes blown by the wind and eroded by the sea, turning it into a fantasy land. The ice under the water gleamed with a life of its own. Fur seals and sea lions lay basking on the bergs, giving us disdainful looks as we drifted past them before lying back down as if it were all too much effort. To be that close to those bergs and to be able to reach out and touch them was just beyond excitement. We clambered back on-board the ship with massive grins that lasted for hours.

The afternoon was rather soured by an unfortunate incident with a whale. The staff on the bridge along with the ever-present 'twitchers' kept a whale watch and informed the rest of us whenever whales came into sight. This usually caused a stampede out on deck to try and film them. On this particular occasion, two humpback whales had been spotted off the bow about half a mile away. We all dashed out and I remember taking photograph after photograph as they got ever closer, with my last photograph taken with me practically hanging off the bow and then BANG! Before we knew it, one whale had crashed into the front – so loudly that people inside could hear it. It was absolutely awful and there was pandemonium as we tried to see what damage we had done. Some said they could see it astern blowing, others said they'd seen lots of blood. We could only console ourselves with the sight of two plumes of water as we motored on regardless.

We were all very subdued that evening asking ourselves, why hadn't the ship changed direction or why hadn't the whale sensed us and moved off? Apparently though, if they are feeding, the humpbacks become oblivious to their surroundings and we were upon it before we could take evasive action. It did raise the question of whether or not we should be down there at all. The Madrid Protocol, ratified in 1991, governs activities in the Antarctic. It determined that only indigenous creatures be allowed in the Antarctic resulting, controversially, in Huskies being removed. On the basis that humans are not indigenous to the region, then strictly speaking we should not be there either and this was the moral dilemma with which we struggled.

Given that we are allowed to visit (and unless we see it, the justification goes, how can we know how important it is that it is preserved), the Antarctic is nevertheless controlled by the Antarctic Treaty which gives very clear guidelines as to what humans can and can't do. This extends to tourists, restricting the numbers of people that can land at any one particular site and the interaction with the local flora and fauna i.e. none.

If you consider that it can take decades for the lichens to grow in that harsh environment, it doesn't take very many heavy-footed humans to destroy all that hard work – it gives a new twist to the saying, 'leave only footprints, take only photographs'. So, it was with rather heavy hearts that we crawled into our berths that night.

There's an odd postscript to this sad tale. All our photographs came out other than the ones I took of the whales. The negatives were totally black for just those five or six pictures – spooky!

We spent the next three days cruising around the Antarctic Peninsula and it was just one fabulous day after another of landing and sitting amongst penguins and elephant seals. Penguins are the most hilarious creatures and caused endless amusement as we watched them waddle about their daily business. They really are not suited to land and they looked so ungainly as they tottered through the snow, marching to and from the sea in their daily quest to feed their young. We had arrived at the tail end of the breeding season and many of the penguins had already left for summer pastures, leaving only those still waiting for their young to moult. And they looked so pathetic huddling against the rocks with bits of feathers dropping off them.

And the smell!!! One thing Sir David Attenborough never tells you about when he's filming these things, is how much they smell. Whilst they are hatching their eggs, they stay exactly where they are and don't move to 'relieve' themselves, so the rocks were covered in red, green and white guano stripes and boy, does it pong. Think of the smell of ammonia from a peroxide bottle, add a hint of rotting seaweed and multiply it tenfold. It really did catch at the back of the throat and thank goodness it was cold. I made the fatal mistake one day of lying down on the ground to film them at penguin level and when I stood up, I was covered head to foot in penguin poo! Alison had to hose me down when we got back on-board, but the smell lingered for days and our cabin took on the distinct aroma of 'perfume de penguin' – thank goodness there were no more rough seas!

The weather was extremely changeable and it was a defining characteristic of the Antarctic. It could be brilliant sunshine one moment and then within minutes, the weather would completely change, the skies would grey over and the wind would whip up out of nowhere. Many of our shore trips were cut short as the weather changed and we had to scramble back on-board the Zodiacs to get back to the relative safety of the ship. We were extremely lucky not to be out on the Drake Passage as we steamed up the channel having heard the news that there was a low pressure belt of epic proportions out in the passage. As it was, the wind howled around the ship as we headed directly into this barrage.

We finally made landing on the Antarctic itself having cruised around Paradise Bay – an immense glacier calving site with huge cathedrals of ice pushing out into the sea. We could hear cracks of thunder all along the coast as icebergs broke off from the land and plunged into the sea.

We were very lucky to see one ourselves during our Antarctic landing at the Almirante Brown Base (Argentinian). We'd climbed up a small hill to survey the surroundings when suddenly, down in the bay in front of our eyes, an iceberg split. I managed to get the video working and caught the second half of the act as it separated and sank below the water and bounced slowly back up, causing waves to roll off it with the Zodiacs darting around it like little fleas as they went up for a closer look. Then suddenly out of nowhere, the wind blew up catching us totally unawares. Fortunately, Bronco had the presence of mind to grab me as I grappled with getting gloves and hat back on whilst fiddling with the camera, before I blew off the edge. All very exciting!

We departed, at last, but not without first getting our passports stamped with the Antarctic stamp.

Then, after four days cruising, the time arrived for our departure from the ship. We had been a great source of interest to the other passengers who were happily living the five-star cruising ship life. We started to shift all our gear out of the holds and pack up the Zodiacs ready for our arrival at Bellingshausen on King George Island. We were aided in this work by a group of young Israeli men (who were travelling the world after completing their national service) for the princely sum of some Mission Antarctic badges. Although I suspect they were actually more interested in impressing our younger and more attractive female expeditioners!

We arrived at King George Island on the most glorious of evenings. The weather was so magnificent, they decided to have an on-deck barbecue. All a bit bizarre, and then even more bizarre, one of the resident lecturers appeared in her bikini, much to the hilarity of the rest of us (but with absolutely no desire to copy her!).

The first Zodiac was filled and departed with most of the team and some of the kit, whilst three of us stayed on-board to supervise the unloading of the last pallets of food and equipment (and in my case, to film the proceedings). After the final boxes had been loaded, we clambered into the Zodiacs after saying our soggy goodbyes to the crew and passengers who had become like family after all our time together.

We were rather quiet, wondering what the next stage of the trip was going to bring – this was the reason why we were here and each of us was lost in silent thought as we motored towards the shore.

JFDI

Our first icebergs!

Hot chocolate and vodka at dawn at the Lemaire Channel aka Kodak Alley

A ship in the Lemaire Channel, to show the scale of the place

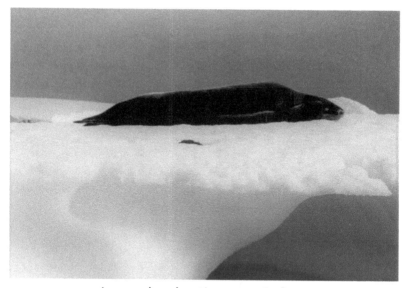

Leopard seal resting on an iceberg

More icebergs!

Gentoo penguin commute #1

Gentoo penguins in their nest

Gentoo penguin commute #2

Rapidly emptying penguin colony

Me filming as a storm comes in – Petermann Island

Almirante Brown Station, Paradise Harbour where the iceberg calved

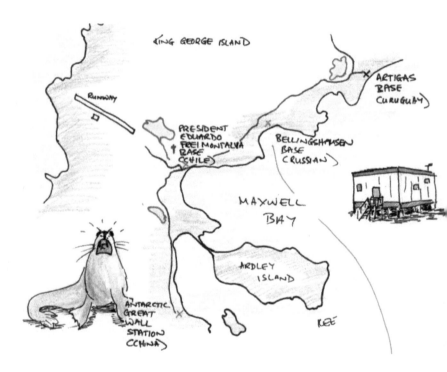

Chapter 5

Bellingshausen – Back of Beyond

*'It does not do to leave a live dragon out of your
calculations, if you live near one.'*
J.R.R. Tolkien, *The Hobbit*

The sight was somewhat daunting as we approached
the shore. The rest of the team stood on the beach
surrounded by a group of silent and morose-
looking Russian men just staring at us. We jumped out
of the boat and before I could catch my breath, a tiny
Russian man came up to me, started jabbering away
excitedly, picked me up and carried me up the beach,
much to the hilarity of the rest of the team.

We stowed our luggage onto an old truck and then
clambered aboard with the small Russian man now
clasping Siaron to his chest, his hands firmly clamped
on her bosom in a less than gentlemanly manner! As we
trundled slowly over the ice shattered pebbles, I spotted
a decrepit old hut standing away from the rest of the
buildings, paint and rust peeling off its square metal
walls. Jokingly, I said to Siaron, 'See that hut, that's ours,

that is,' and we both chortled, safe in the knowledge that it couldn't possibly be our accommodation. The giggles rather quickly dried up as the lorry pulled up outside this excuse for a building and the realisation dawned – it actually is ours!

Once again, a shell-shocked team timidly entered the building to view our new home. Suddenly our tiny on-board cabins seemed like 5-star-luxury as we stared into the gloom and took in the dark walls and sparse furniture.

Thank goodness for Bronco as he marshalled us into activity. He split us into rooms – women into one and men into another. We found some rather dubious mattresses rolled up which we dragged off and chose our own floor space on which to lay them. Three of them chose to stay at ground level whilst I picked the sleeping platform accessed by a steep ladder – you take what privacy you can.

Then there was the 'kitchen'. Another room except this one had some cupboards into which we stashed all our provisions and banged nails into one of the overhead beams with an ice axe to hang our mugs. No sink, no taps, no oven, just cupboards. Luckily, Bronco had brought a kettle with him, so at least we could have tea and coffee (but boil the water three times before using it!). There was also a sleeping platform in there where Richard made his home.

The 'lounge' contained all our blue barrels, one fold-out sun lounger (the sofa), a set of wooden stairs propped against the wall (the bookshelves) and a small desk with our laptop (the office).

Saving the best to last – the 'bathroom'! Apologies for all the quotation marks, but these terms are relative and to suggest that these rooms bore any resemblance to what we know as kitchens, lounges and bathrooms back in the UK would be a gross misrepresentation. Back to the 'bathroom'; this consisted of a sink with a cold water tap and a separate glory hole containing the 'toilet'. The toilet was a box with a wooden seat covering a large hole down into a tank – no need for flushing here. All very sanitary – not!

Thankfully, we were in the Antarctic and it was cold, because after a few days, this thing started filling up rapidly and the smell increased correspondingly. By the end of our stay, when it still hadn't been emptied, it had reached its capacity and was no longer useable. Being right by the front door, this was a great way to welcome people to our humble abode as they dashed past the noisome smell before making their way into our lounge. I remember writing one report back to the UK, discussing this subject at length. But as I wrote at the time, when the line between basic and primitive becomes blurred, these things take on great significance.

The difference between the men's and women's rooms was hilarious. Most of the men had decided to sleep on camp beds all in a row with their kit beside their beds. Our room in contrast had been transformed – we had a washing line up, little knick-knacks adorned one corner shelving unit and we even boasted a drinks cabinet – our nesting instincts not to be ignored.

Within an hour of arriving, a couple of French men stumbled into our cabin thinking we were the new trade store and had stopped by to purchase cigarettes from us. Quite what they were doing there was never explained – we never saw them again and goodness only knows what they thought of us. Our entire two weeks there was peppered with strange happenings like this and were great sources of amusement to us.

Within two hours of arriving, a contingent from the Uruguayan base, Artigas, had arrived! They'd seen the ship arriving and had immediately leapt into a vehicle and driven the five miles across lunar-like landscape to check us out. You can imagine their great excitement to discover four women, and within minutes of their arrival we had been invited to a party on Saturday night! Bearing in mind that we were the only females amongst a total of about 100 men scattered about various bases, we were of huge interest and you could almost smell the testosterone!

By 11pm, we were finished and after taking some much-needed wine (we weren't totally devoid of creature comforts!), we crawled gratefully into our sleeping bags, eager to see what tomorrow brought.

I managed to sleep through the others getting up, and at 8 o'clock I hurriedly threw some clothes on top of my thermals and ran down to the main hut to have breakfast. Our meals were taken 20 minutes after the Russians so we didn't get in their way. But, of course, their curiosity was as great as ours, so we had a reception party awaiting us. They were still as daunting in the morning and I tiptoed in feeling very self-conscious, very aware that all eyes were upon me as I shrugged off my jacket in the hallway. In order to keep some semblance of tidiness, we had to take our boots off to stop trailing in mud. The Russians had an assortment of slippers lined up and very kindly, they insisted we wore them when we came in. I schlepped into the dining room wearing outsize slippers and tried to work out the system, not helped by being silently watched by these brooding men in their odd assortment of clothing.

The dining room was a throwback to the 1950s with drab walls and plain trestle tables and a television with a scratchy picture blaring out in the corner. Having discovered the plates and cutlery, I walked over to the serving hatch to sample the delights of the Russian buffet breakfast.

This was breakfast, the likes of which I never wanted to see again. Somehow the chef contrived to extract all semblance of colour and taste out of the food and turned it into an unidentifiable shapeless mess of grey hideousness. Breakfast was, in fact, generally the best meal of the day, but I took one look at it and my appetite vanished. After prodding about for a while, I eventually settled on a slice of bread and what looked like cold tea from a large metal bucket. This was actually just about drinkable until one day I made the mistake of stirring the bucket with the ladle and dark shapes floated up from the bottom before sinking back down into obscurity. I have absolutely no idea what it was, but clearly it wasn't tea!

Every mealtime was a magical mystery tour and kept us intellectually stimulated as we tried to work out what ingredients had been mangled at the hands of the chef. It was unremitting in its awfulness. To be fair to the chef, he was the only cook on-site and had no backup. So, for 13 months (or 395 days if you prefer), he had to cook breakfast, lunch and dinner without a single day off. He must have been bored and exhausted.

All the food is supplied at the beginning of the season and is put into a freezer. The only fresh food they ever ate, was the bread that 'cheffie' baked daily. He was on his second tour of duty and on the first tour he had apparently gone around the bend. And he chose to come back… What was more incredible was that they allowed him back! I later heard that he went back for a third tour!

Amongst other provisions, we had brought US$5,000 worth of fresh food for them, including 100 kilos of chicken, 500 kilos of potatoes, onions, cabbage, beet and carrots, 15 dozen eggs, salami, milk, cheese, fruit and beer. Did we ever see any of it? I think we had apples on one day, a very small green salad another and chicken a couple of times (as much as I could identify it), but beyond that, whence the food had gone remained a complete mystery.

When you're stuck in the middle of nowhere for months on end, isolated from the world, food is so vital for keeping up morale. It was no wonder the Russians always looked so grey and morose; you would too with disgusting slop on your plates for 13 months at a stretch. Forget Michelin stars and Good Food Guides, we invented a new scale for assessing the edibility of food and one that I'm surprised has not yet been instigated globally. It is the Bellingshausen Base where 0 is Bellingshausen food and everything else can be compared against this absolute zero of the cooking world.

Luckily for us, we had brought a load of food for the hut consisting mainly of biscuits, chocolate, nuts, dried fruit and cheese so at least we could escape and top up on calories clandestinely in the hut. Even so, we weren't without our own culinary mishaps. Unfortunately, the cheese and some of the biscuits had been stored in the same barrel as an outboard engine and diesel and they had absorbed the distinct flavour of petroleum which was pretty vile. Nevertheless, it got eaten. Desperate times…

There was a great bonus to the Antarctic in the chocolate department for me. Because the weather is so changeable, you can never take any risks, even when it looks lovely out. This meant that every time we went out anywhere, we had to go in pairs, and we also had to take food with us just in case disaster struck and we got stranded. So off we would go with chocolate and nuts stuffed into our jackets. Licence to eat chocolate – I was in heaven. An even greater bonus was that instead of the food I wasn't eating at the base canteen, I was eating chocolates and biscuits like they were going out of fashion to compensate and I was still losing weight! It's a long way to go and a rather drastic way of shedding pounds, but it worked for me.

And boy, did the Russians love our biscuits! We probably don't even notice the volume of chocolates and biscuits as they're everywhere and part of our everyday lives in the Western world. But to the Russians, our simple chocolate biscuits were like gold dust. We had a constant stream of visitors, all conveniently arriving at around teatime (some British institutions being maintained at all costs). It was a joy to see them sitting on the barrels with up to three packets of different biscuits on their laps because they couldn't choose which ones they wanted.

Once the horror of our first breakfast was out of the way, Bronco shooed us all out of the hut so that he could swear and curse away in peace whilst trying to get the satellite link established with the UK. A few of the Russians decided to take us on a tour of the base and then for a walk around the nearby Ardley Island, accessible at low tide by a spit.

JFDI

'Gruntly and Charmless', our home at Bellingshausen

Making tea in the 'kitchen'

Sleeping quarters (men's on the left, women's on the right)

Bellingshausen food – as modelled by Chris!

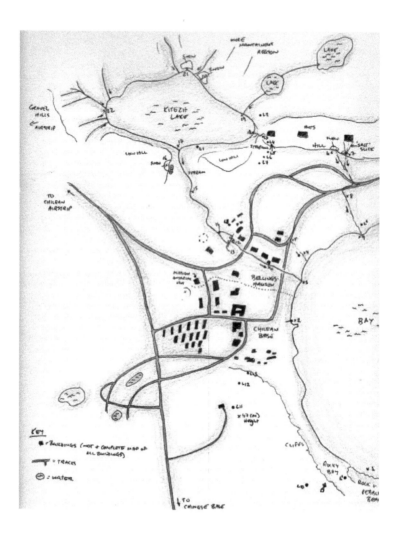

Chapter 6

Exploring 62 Degrees South

'It's opener, out there, in the wide, open air.'
Dr Seuss, *Oh, The Places You'll Go!*

The base itself was sited on the shore – a few meagre run-down orange and green huts (looking for all the world like the container vessels you see on ships) connected by wooden decking (the likes of which Alan Titchmarsh would shudder at). Electric cables were strung between the huts and rusted metal pipes stuck out of the ground at random angles seemingly going nowhere. On the beach was a huge pile consisting of scrap metal, barrels, containers and even an old lorry. This was a collection of all the waste that had been scattered around the base over decades of habitation there and was the reason behind Mission Antarctica. It was funding a team of Russian men who lived on the base for six months of the year and who were breaking up the scrap and bringing it to the shore for removal in 2001 (eventually delayed to 2002).

In contrast, the Chilean base was immediately next door on the shore and the difference between the two bases could not be starker. Their base was almost a village. White painted buildings with gaily coloured corrugated roofing which included a gym, a bank, a post office, a science block, a school and a whole row of living huts. The gym was immense with a full-size basketball court and showers (which we coveted). There was even a bright blue church with proper pews and an altar! The Chileans knew how to do Antarctic surveying in style to the extent that they also brought their wives and children with them for the summer season. They even boasted an airstrip up on the hilltop.

A few miles down the coast was a Chinese base and, as mentioned, the Uruguayan base five miles off in the other direction. It was a popular island for bases due to the fact that a lot of the ice melted off during the summer season.

What always mystified me was that they each had their own scientists and meteorologists all collecting similar data on the Antarctic or weather conditions. Why they didn't combine their skills only dawned on me when I realised that there was a huge amount of vested interest in maintaining bases down there. At the moment and until 2048 when the Antarctic Treaty gets renegotiated (hopefully), the Antarctic belongs to no one. This hasn't stopped countries from staking their claims and the whole continent is already sliced up, by nation, in readiness for the day it comes up for grabs.

Whilst we were there, we bumped into some Peruvian officials visiting (along with their Bolivian pilot!) who had flown into the Chilean base en route to their base. Their base is opened at the beginning of the summer season by a maintenance team. A few scientists pop along, take a few measurements and look busy until the officials come along to inspect. Having seen that their money is being spent wisely, they would then fly off home ready to sign the budget for the next year. The scientists then pack up and off they go, happy in the knowledge that they can repeat the exercise next year and get paid handsomely to carry on! Madness.

Anyhow, I'm digressing again. Having 'oohed' and 'aahed' at the Russian base, we were frogmarched off to the island at speed where we were immediately accosted by a very cross sea lion. They are very scary beasts if roused and can move at quite a pace when defending themselves. I was horrified at the cruelty as the Russians chased after it bashing rocks together laughing all the while. I know they were trying to make sure we were safe, but I would rather have not gone to the island than cause distress to the local wildlife. I was also completely paranoid about the moss and lichens and it took me an age to get anywhere. I was so determined I was not going to knowingly kill any and I seethed quietly as others seemed happy to march on regardless, despite my desperate pleas to watch where they were walking.

The Antarctic is very bleak during the summer without its splendid ice covering. Other than my precious lichens and mosses, nothing grows there. It's a barren landscape with ice shattered rock underfoot and tall, craggy rocky outcrops covered with the last of the nesting penguins and the layer of (still very smelly) guano. We finally returned via the clifftops where we stopped to look at a particularly beautiful monument to some lost sailors. The coastline is peppered with crosses where people have succumbed to the harsh environs of the continent and were a constant reminder that the Antarctic is not to be taken lightly.

The views from the cliffs were magnificent. We could see for miles across the water to other glacier capped islands and catch glimpses of icebergs out to sea. It is so much clearer down there due to the lack of pollution meaning that what seems like only a couple of miles back home is actually more like 10 miles – it was very confusing on the eyes! It also gave us a bird's-eye view of what was to be our home for the next two weeks, and it looked grim!

We slid back to the Chilean base down a steep escarpment and returned back to our hut, which Richard had decided looked like a biscuit tin and had christened Huntley and Palmers (and which I promptly renamed Gruntly and Charmless). Bronco had been successful in setting up the satellite link and we now had communication back home – hurrah!

Before we left, we had to decide whether or not we wanted to hear bad news from home. On the basis there wouldn't be very much that could be done if indeed there was any bad news, I decided that I didn't want to know. In fact, I'd also decided that I didn't really want to know anything about what was going on in the outside world – I wanted to experience the Antarctic without external distractions.

As it was, we could only communicate via OSB to save clogging the airwaves with emails from friends and families, and that suited me just fine. Each day we would take it in turns to write the daily report which got typed up and squirted back to the UK to selected people, and it was something I always looked forward to doing and would quite happily have written them all had I been given the opportunity.

JFDI

Bellingshausen base with the Chilean one (Frei) behind

Our hut

'Shop Russian'

Bellingshausen Russian
Base

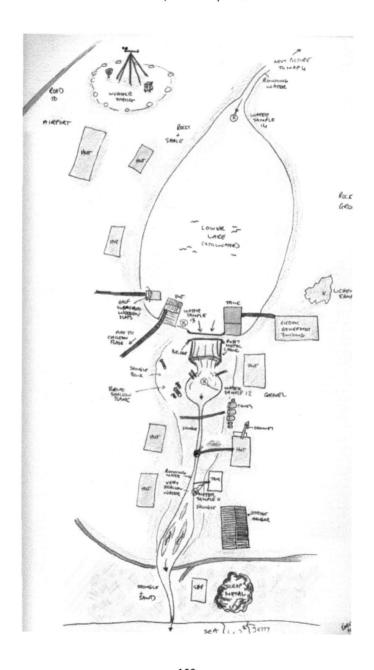

Chapter 7

Life on the Edge of the World

'Today was good. Today was fun. Tomorrow is another one.'
Dr Seuss, *One Fish, Two Fish, Red Fish, Blue Fish*

After a quick brew, it was down to some work. At my pre-expedition meeting with Bronco, he had asked me to take on a project for the Water Research Council. I had duly gone to meet them and picked up all my kit to carry out the research. Essentially, they wanted to test out a new water sampling methodology, one that would be easily transportable to anywhere in the world. This seemed like a simple enough project having read the instructions, but actually dominated my and Alison's day to day activities for the duration of the stay.

In essence, we had to collect water samples from a number of different sites around the base, take a GPS measurement to pinpoint the exact spot that we had collected it from, transfer them to small syringe barrels and return them to the UK for testing. Sounds easy, doesn't it, from the comfort of your chair? Ha!

There were a couple of immediate problems, the first being a lack of alcohol. I had been given a jar of ethanol as part of the kit, but when I asked at the check-in back in the UK they had taken it off me as being a dangerous substance. The ethanol was used to 'charge' a wad of cotton in the bottom of the barrels before we put the water into them. So, where to find a source of neat alcohol? Of course, it's a Russian base, the place must be swimming in the stuff! Unfortunately, Oleg, the base commander, ran a dry base – no alcohol to be consumed. This was a very sensible strategy given the high boredom factor of the place and the inherent risks of getting drunk in the middle of the Antarctic. Luckily though, he did have a secret supply and after some careful negotiation, he measured out a small amount and gave it to us, insisting that we return whatever was unused.

Having overcome that problem, we then had the GPS problem. As part of my research, we were supposed to accurately pinpoint where we were taking samples from by using a GPS (global positioning system) device. Did we have a GPS? Did the Russians have a GPS? Did the Russians have a map resembling anything approaching an OS map. No, to all three!

A Plan B was needed. The only thing I could think of was to try and draw maps as accurately as possible and to photograph the sample locations making sure there were identifying landmarks in the picture enabling future sample takers to find the spot. Taking Alison with me, off we went to try and find a range of suitable water spots covering as many different water types as possible. We spent a good couple of hours wandering along the shoreline, up streams and around a lake up behind the Russian camp, marking locations on rough maps as we went.

We were also supposed to collect lichen samples in the same spots, but this also proved to be very tricky as a) we weren't entirely sure what lichens looked like and b) the vegetation we saw that we thought was lichens was growing so closely against the rocks, that scraping them off resulted in heaps of powder, causing us great concern.

We went back to the hut and sent an email off to the Water Research Council and sat back to await enlightenment. No response... so we had to work it out for ourselves.

In the meantime, Chris, the headmaster, had disappeared off with Nat in tow, collecting information for his educational website that he was hoping to develop for use in Cumbria. Alex had wandered off to start taking measurements of the buildings for her project to try and get wind turbines into Bellingshausen as an eco-friendly option to the diesel on which the site was run.

Then it was time to spruce up for the party at Artigas. But not before the next concoction cooked up by chef – some form of ravioli and a dessert of a quasi doughnut with condensed milk. The Russians then piled us onto one of their amphibian trucks and we jolted and lurched across the few miles to the Uruguayan base in high excitement, leaving Bronco and Richard behind for a quiet night in.

What a difference a base can make. The Uruguayan mess was worlds apart from the Russian base. Light coloured wooden panelling, a good telly and lots of videos. And food glorious food – buckets of the stuff. Pizzas, cheese nibbles, cherries, olives, hot dogs – fantastic. Then there was drink – stuff to blow your head off, which I managed to mostly avoid other than to take timid sips when I was forced to.

The evening started off rather awkwardly as our Spanish and their English was pretty ropy, and I was very glad of the smattering of Spanish I'd picked up when in Madrid visiting friends. After a couple of drinks, one of the men (a Wessex helicopter pilot trained in Taunton and Wales!) got out his guitar and gave us his (unusual) renditions of Rod Stewart and Elton John! Then without further ado, they pushed all the tables out of the way, put on the stereo and the serious dancing started.

What fun! Real Latino dancing – thank goodness for my Ceroc lessons, I knew they'd pay off one day – and I spent the evening in a whirl being thrown around the room by a variety of increasingly drunk and amorous Uruguayans. It was fantastic! The South American men love dancing and, unlike their British counterparts who need at least 10 pints before even contemplating a drunken shuffle, they were up the minute the music started.

Finally, at goodness knows what time, we squeezed into the back of a truck and drove back at what felt like breakneck speed to Bellingshausen.

The whole evening had felt surreal – there I was, in the middle of the Antarctic, eating pizza, drinking wine and dancing the salsa. You couldn't make this stuff up!

The next morning, as you might imagine, was a bit of a slow start and when I finally woke up at about nine, I decided it was time to have my first 'bath'. So, armed with my towel and baby wipes, I headed off into the little girls' room. Bathing Antarctic style in our hut meant taking off one layer at a time, gritting your teeth and having a very hurried strip wash in cold water. No luxuriating in baths of hot bubble bath for us! Baby wipes and panty liners were a godsend as washing self and clothes was not an easy operation. You may well grimace and think how disgusting, but trust me, washing knickers was not easy and panty liners were a relatively hygienic option!!!

Once in a slightly more sanitary state, Richard then followed me and Alison out to film us taking water samples. After an hour of this, we then headed back for a brew (the days were punctuated by a lot of brews and quick chats before heading back out to carry on with our jobs). Just as we were about to go out again, the Uruguayans popped in; some to see our female colleagues, who had been very popular indeed, others to offer us a shower up at Artigas and better still, to invite us to another party on the following Saturday. We all looked to Bronco expectantly and he gave us the official OK, much to everyone's delight.

It was fascinating to see how the group dynamics were emerging. We were this eclectic bunch from very different backgrounds which resulted in some interesting team dynamics. Bronco was completely focused on the logistics of organising the removal of the waste in the following year and spent many hours in meetings with Oleg to work out how it was all going to happen. The rest of us were busy doing our own thing, so during the days we spent little time with each other.

Alex and I didn't hit it off – she had a magnetism that seemed to blind a lot of men rendering them incapable of seeing beyond her beauty and she told an excellent story. Being totally honest with myself, I know it was just green-eyed jealousy – men very rarely hang on my every word, and as a consequence, I've always prided myself on advancing myself based on my competence and humour rather than my looks. So, her behaviour and men's reactions to it annoyed me beyond belief. It started on-board the ship as men just listened to her with their mouths open and metaphorically dribbling and later once we reached Bellingshausen. This says more about men than it does about Alex, and who can blame her if it works – I'd probably do it too if it worked for me.

But as time went on, it dawned on some of us, that whilst she was passionate about achieving global eco-friendliness, she did not appear to have the pragmatism to go with it and she seemed unable to translate that passion into reality. It was as if she didn't really know how to make notes and take measurements accurately.

Siaron, on the other hand, was a godsend to me, being the nearest in age as well as a closet smoker, and we spent many a time shivering on the steps smoking and having a good old natter.

Richard had been initially enchanted by Alex, but unfortunately for her, she crossed him in one area where none of us would have dared to tread. He was a chain smoker and we had never established smoking rules within the hut, which in retrospect we should have done. So, we were rather selfishly smoking in the hut (it was quite parky outside after all). Rather than take Richard to one side and have a quiet chat with him, she went to Bronco and complained about it, which, of course, was within her rights to do so, but perhaps was not the best option to take. Poor Bronco then had the unenviable task of broaching the subject with Richard. I returned to the hut one afternoon to find Richard in high dudgeon and steaming mad. It took ages to winkle the truth out of him, but winkle it I did. From that point on, until we left for our glacier trip, Richard spent the entire time in the hut, hidden away on his sleeping platform smoking feverishly and muttering darkly and nothing could be done to cheer him up. This made life in the hut distinctly uncomfortable for some of us. Luckily, Chris was too thick-skinned to notice and remained bluff and cheerful and Nat, who had become his quiet sidekick, remained as inscrutable as ever. We only managed to salvage the situation by relocating a comfy chair from the dining hut one night and supplying him with gin and tonic before we headed off on our walk.

In spite of these tensions, the days settled into a comfortable pattern. Get up, have breakfast, go out and collect water samples with Alison, back for tea, more samples, lunch, transfer samples to small barrels, type up notes, tea, and so on.

Collecting water samples though involved risking life and limb against sea lions and irate skuas. Skuas are large predatory birds with very sharp claws and hooked beaks (think brown seagulls on steroids!).

Their proximity made the research a reasonably perilous exercise. If you got too close to a skua nest, they became very agitated and would try to scare you off. They did this by dive-bombing you and squealing menacingly as they did so. If that didn't work, they would try Plan B which was to try and bomb you with guano as they dived down. Considering that they had a wingspan of nearly six feet, you can imagine it was quite intimidating.

On one particularly scary occasion up at the lake, we were trying to walk round it to reach our last collection point rather than having to go all the way back, when we were attacked again. I had read somewhere that skuas are actually a bit stupid and will attack the highest point, so we had found some planks and were wandering along using these as distractions. Feeling suddenly much braver, we thought we'd try and get some good photos of them dive-bombing us, so we marched on obviously getting ever closer to their nesting sites hidden amongst the rocks. We then spent a very scary half hour scrambling along the shoreline with an increasingly irate pair of skuas swooping down on us. Having got beyond the point of no return, we just had to continue until we got past the danger zone. There was a lot of nervous giggling having reached the safety of a beach. Don't try this at home, kids!

Another collection site had to be abandoned when we stumbled across a sea lion's resting place. They are cunningly camouflaged and I hadn't seen him as I walked along the shoreline and hurriedly retraced my steps backwards as he suddenly emerged barking at me and bearing his fangs.

Notwithstanding the scary nature of the work, I was finding it extremely satisfying. I had been given a task to do, and I was doing it well. We were collecting a lot of really useful feedback and we were meticulous in our record keeping and produced a fantastic report between us, complete with hand-drawn maps and accurate data. It proved to me that I could actually deliver something on time and to a high standard in a way that work back at the office couldn't. It went a long way to restoring some faith in myself.

After our hairy morning with the skuas and sea lion, the Uruguayans paid us a very welcome visit and offered us showers up at Artigas. We jumped at the opportunity, quickly grabbing our wash kits, clean knickers, socks and shirts.

When we got there, the Chinese had beaten us to it and were having a briefing session on glaciology before being taken for a helicopter ride. It's a real 'scratch my back and I'll scratch yours' world down there. The Chileans have the runway and post office, the Uruguayans the helicopter and the Chinese the bulldozer. Quite what the Russians brought to the party was unclear and I think was one of the reasons the Russians had problems socialising with the other bases because they had nothing to share in return.

As usual, we were treated like royalty. We were shown to the infirmary for our showers and what bliss to be able to wash off several days' worth of grime. However, unluckily for Siaron, who wasn't feeling very well, the hot water ran out by the time she got there and she had to make do with cold.

Once we were cleaned up, we went and had tea with the Uruguayan chief, Major Waldemar Fontes. He had arrived in November and was overwintering for the first time with 11 other staff to keep the station ticking over during the dark months. I hadn't realised that they all had to undergo psychological profiling before they came to the base to try and minimise the risk of going stir-crazy during 24-hour darkness. It made a lot of sense, especially once I returned and kept in email contact with a Chilean meteorologist whose emails became increasingly odd through the winter period.

We had a long talk with them about whether the Antarctic was shrinking due to global warming and as ever, when the subject is discussed, the opinions varied wildly. One said that the glacier had shrunk to 280 metres from 340 metres in the last nine years, whereas another said it had actually only shrunk a few centimetres. What you cannot argue with is the data. An article I was given by one of the scientists on-board the ship showed that the nesting sites of different types of penguin was changing, which reflected the different nature of the Antarctic conditions as it warmed up. It all seems quite alarming that wholesale changes are taking place (such as the sheering of the ice sheet the size of Somerset earlier that year) and we carry on regardless, even now, over twenty years later!

In the meantime, some of the other girls were receiving attention from the males and I sighed to myself – so much for meeting Mr Right – I couldn't even succeed being one of only four females amongst 100 men! Hardly surprising though, given that I had my professional hat on and was probably wafting off subconscious waves to that end. I had cut my hair short prior to the trip, and had brought no make-up or perfume with me unlike the others, because I was so determined to be a 'proper' adventurer.

We got back to Gruntly and Charmless at about 6.30 with the atmosphere still fraught with tension and added chagrin with a message from Standard Life saying they hadn't had any reports from Alison which caused her great concern. Ah, the joys of close confinement living.

JFDI

Skua avoidance tactics

DRAKE PASSAGE

ROCKY POINT

ARCTOWSKI ICEFIELD

BELLINGSHAUSEN   × ARTIGAS

ELEPHANT SEALS MOULTING

Chapter 8

Glaciers and Gales

'We need the tonic of wildness.'
Henry David Thoreau, *Walden*

Luckily, before the situation exploded we were distracted by our impending ice walk. As part of the trip, we were going to spend a couple of days camping out on the ice and Bronco got us all busy in making preparations. The blue barrels were reopened and out came the rucksacks, ice boots, crampons and ice axes.

The Russians thought we were completely mad and offered to drive us up the road to the drop-off point some five miles away. Bronco resisted for a while, but then decided that discretion was the better part of valour and finally agreed to the lift. I was furious. I had been looking forward to this physical challenge having been denied my Drake Passage sail. I knew I was going to find it hard work not having done any serious walking in my time, but I wanted to see if I could do it without complaining too much.

The morning arrived, very overcast with a murky fog cloaking the base. Siaron and I had been muttering together about the transport and as we were loading the truck up with our rucksacks, I mustered my courage and sidled up to Bronco to ask him if it would be OK if Siaron and I walked to the site. His brow furrowed and he got a steely glint in his eyes and I thought, 'Oh no, I've insulted him now'. Then he looked at me and said, 'Oh sod it, I'm going to walk too!'. And that was it; off came the rucksacks and we cheerfully lugged them on to our backs laden with our kit: sleeping bag, Thermarest, bag liner, ice boots, crampons, harness slings with carabiners, bivvy bag, change of thermals, spare hat and gloves, goggles, Thermos flasks (full), book, notebook, loo roll, head torch, nappy liners, suntan lotion, Nivea, toothbrush, penknife, bars of chocolate, nuts, sultanas, coffee sachets, eye mask and ear plugs (very essential items when sharing a tent with three others). All that is except for Alex, who had a bad knee and would prefer to take the offered lift. Richard also declined to join us, preferring the relative comfort of the hut with his comfy chair and stash of gin and cigarettes. He gaily waved us off, his good mood almost restored.

Very soon, the base disappeared in the swirling mists as we started our long trudge up the side of the hill along the road that led to Artigas. I was soon lagging behind the main group but quietly determined to not make a fuss and taking a small measure of comfort from Nat, who was struggling along even further behind me.

We finally made it to the turning off point and waited for Alex to arrive before heading off the road to our campsite. Such was the kindness of the driver that he took the lorry off road and dropped her off within a hundred yards of the campsite whilst we sweated along under the weight of our rucksacks.

We set up camp with Bronco and Siaron taking charge of erecting the tents. Given the prevailing winds, we set up the tents with the entrance facing away from the wind to give us some protection, weighted the edges down with rocks and then went off to practice ice falls with our crampons and ice axes.

We strapped on the crampons and ascended onto the glacier, stomping purposefully to allow the spikes to gain purchase in the ice. Having reached a suitably steep slope, Bronco then took us through our paces showing us how to stop should we lose our grip whilst walking to prevent a headlong slide to the bottom (or worse, over the edge of a crevasse).

Having successfully managed this, we trudged back to the campsite for dinner. Sensibly, the men opted for soup and crackers, but we decided on a culinary feast of pasta and soya reconstituted meat sauce. Our fatal mistake was to cook the pasta first so by the time we came to eat it, it had dissolved into a mess of white soggy slush – yet another ruined meal!

The men had one tent and the women shared the other and it was cosy to say the least. We were packed in like sardines, head to toe with our kit at our heads as pillows. Deep joy, I slept next to Alex who spent half the night sprawled over me, leaving me very little space! It was pretty chilly and we slept fully dressed and I tied up the drawstrings of the sleeping bag to keep the chill off my face. I woke up several hours later in a complete claustrophobic panic, convinced I was suffocating and sat bolt upright whilst I disentangled myself. Once my beating heart had returned to normal, I fell back into a fitful sleep, only to be woken what felt like moments later, with Chris bellowing cheerfully at us to get up. This man was made for the outdoors and early rising. He was striding about in his shirt sleeves whilst I shivered under several hundred layers of clothing.

We had a quick brew, made up some flasks with hot orange, packed small day sacks to share between two of us and set off once again for the glacier.

We had Valerie with us, the lead Russian from the Ryazan team, and the contrast between ourselves and him was hilarious. There we were, all decked out in our North Face jackets, ice boots, crampons and ice axes and he had on a pair of Wellington boots, a parka coat, some cheap sunglasses and a wooden walking stick!

I was also lugging the video camera, all wrapped up in a sleeping bag cover to protect it. Bronco was rather unsure about it, but Richard had insisted that he wanted the walk filmed and had given me very explicit instructions on how to keep continuity, so it was my burden to carry it, filming as I went.

The walk to the top of the glacier couldn't have taken much more than an hour, but it was really hard going, and the enormity of undertaking to walk across Antarctica and to have to keep walking for eight hours a day, never mind pulling a sled behind you, started to dawn on me. I spoke to Bronco about this endless slogging and he responded saying that one thing he hated was the festering in tents for days on end while waiting for the weather to break. On asking him why he did it, he merely shrugged his shoulders saying that there was always a new mountain top to reach.

Then, in the middle of nowhere, we came across a whole load of wooden pallets and bird carcasses and we could only assume they had dropped out of an airplane as there was no other obvious explanation.

On reaching the top of the glacier, we were rewarded with the most fantastic panoramic views across King George Island and out to other islands, the sea dotted with icebergs.

We descended the glacier across small crevasses having been assured by Bronco that there was only a very small risk of there being larger ones. Nevertheless, I was very quick at leaping over the foot-wide gaps, taking care not to look down the breaks in the ice. We finally reached the edge of the glacier where it hit the sea and we were struck once again by the beauty of the ice. The cliff of ice soared up for a few hundred feet and was layered like a sponge cake where a volcano had erupted on another island and laid down ash at 10-year intervals.

Having settled ourselves down on the rocky shore for some lunch (nuts and chocolate mostly), the wind started to get up and the wave tops were getting blown off as it rose. Deciding not to linger any longer, we began the long walk back along the shore with the wind starting to tug at us.

It was all rather precarious as the shore was littered with great clumps of elephant seals just lying around piled up against each other grunting whilst they moulted. If possible, the smell they created was even worse than the penguins and if you got too close to them, they lifted their huge heads and opened their great mouths revealing pink mouths and rather nasty looking teeth. However, they were the least of our worries with a few sea lions around, who would charge us as soon as they saw us. It was quite tricky as you are not supposed to get between them and their escape route – the sea in this instance – but there was no other way through and I just hoped they couldn't sense my fear.

After what seemed like ages, we came across a small hut propped up on whale bones and we stopped for a small break, relieved to get out of the wind for a few minutes. It contained nothing more than two sleeping bunks and a visitors' book and was used by the Russians to come fishing. We left a bar of chocolate and wrote messages in the book before continuing along our way.

The group then split up with some of us deciding to continue along the coast whilst the others took the high route over the cliffs. By now the wind was a howling gale and I was unable to make much headway, spending more time being blown sideways to the sea than going forward. Alison was astounding; she marched on laughing at me whilst I tottered off in all directions other than the one I wanted, up until the point her hat blew off into a pool of water.

Eventually Valerie got fed up with me and grabbed me by the arm and frogmarched me along helpless beside him. I was in a right mess by this stage. Because I was in Valerie's grip, I couldn't blow my nose which was streaming snot at the rate of what felt like a litre a minute and with the wind it was being blown out horizontally. Unfortunately, Alison, who was walking beside Valerie to get some protection from the wind, bore the full brunt of my nostril contents down the front of her jacket!!!

How pleased was I to see the campsite?! I tottered in and Alison and I got the Trangia lit to make a brew for the others who were behind us. During the day, the wind had veered around by 180 degrees and was now blowing straight into our tent – so much for our careful planning. There was very little else to do in the wind, and cooking dinner was out of the question, so we crawled into the tents for some high-level festering at about 5pm.

The tent was battered by the winds and the noise was incredible and there was nothing to do except sit in our sleeping bags and chat loudly over the sound of the wind. So there we were, busy doing nothing, when suddenly there was a scratching at the entrance and in popped one of the lads from the Russian base! They had taken pity on us and marched in the increasing gloom and gales across the hills to deliver some food to us! It was very welcome even though, as per usual, there was no way of guessing what it was.

They finally left us and it was back to festering again. We decided to draw straws to see who would have to go to the toilet first as we had been putting it off for hours, but it was getting to the point of discomfort by about 9 and someone had to make a break for it. Siaron went off first and blew back in a few minutes later and then it was my turn. This is no easy task as a woman. Not only do you have many layers on, you cannot leave toilet paper around so it had to be collected and returned to base. So off I went, clutching loo paper and a nappy sack, in search of a spot out of the wind. I finally found somewhere relatively wind free and began the delayering process.

When it's that cold, you pee as fast as you possibly can (having also made sure that the wind was behind you) before your nether regions start to freeze! I managed to look up briefly and my breath was taken away by the beauty of the scenery. The sun was almost but not quite setting over the sea with a small lake in front of me being blasted by the wind. But having done the deed, I didn't linger and staggered back to the relative warmth of the tent.

After another uncomfortable night, once again Chris brought us sharply back to the land of the living at the crack of sparrows and it was time to break camp and head back to Bellingshausen taking the scenic route.

The wind had died down slightly overnight, but it was still a challenge getting the tents down and Alison ended up lying across ours as we collapsed it to save it from being blown away.

Having cleared up, we hoisted up our rucksacks again and headed off across country. Alex had barely gone 100 yards before she complained, and before you knew it Bronco had taken her rucksack off her and walked off with it balanced on top of his! Valerie was either tired, I'd become miraculously fit overnight, or he had decided to take pity on us (the latter, I feel) because he slowed down his punishing pace enough to allow us to stop and admire the view. It was the most fantastic morning – the sun was shining and everywhere about us were little lakes which had frozen overnight. I remember climbing one small hill and turned around to take in the scenery. I had what can only be described as a near-religious moment. The Drake Passage was off to the left, sprinkled with icebergs, the glacier gleaming bright white to my right with the desolate landscapes and lakes in front of me and skuas wheeling overhead. It was so unspoilt and perfect with no sign of human habitation that I became overwhelmed with a feeling of total peace and well-being. Everything was very right with the world for that brief moment.

Actually, it was an extension of what I had been feeling generally. Being on King George Island was so far removed from the real world that I thought of nothing other than the experience of being there. Occasionally an image of family would float through my head, but then just drift off again. It's a real lesson in mindfulness, of just being present in the moment without thinking of anything else beyond that moment. Even though it was an enforced isolation, the inability to be in touch with my normal reality made it a delicious slice of not having to think.

I haven't felt so at peace with myself before or since. Which tells me my journey is far from over. I've not yet found my place in the world or sufficient happiness with myself and acceptance and celebration of who I am.

After a couple of hours, we made it back to the escarpment leading back down to Bellingshausen, and what a sight lay before us. With the winds, the bay had been filled up with trash ice and the shoreline was white with large lumps of ice. With the sun shining and rimmed as it was with the ice, the base actually looked quite pretty. We slid down the slope and wended our weary way back through the base and to the hut to be greeted by Richard and his video camera.

Whilst we'd been gone, he'd been having his own little adventures. He'd attempted to get to the food hut the night before, but the wind had been so strong he'd got blown over and decided rather sensibly to stick to a liquid diet back in Gruntly and Charmless. The Russians were concerned for his welfare and he'd had a steady stream of them coming past to check he was OK and insisting that he ate. The last two, Vladimir and Vladimir (I jest not!) arrived bearing a gift of an apple each for him. You will not be surprised to hear that they were left sitting in the kitchen (the apples, not the Russians).

To return their kindness, he invited them in for a wee drop of whisky which they had never tasted before. An hour and a half later, they tottered off – typical Richard hospitality strikes again. Having finally gone to bed, the wind was howling through a vent in the kitchen so he eventually got up to try and close it. The vent sits about 10 feet up from the floor above the kitchen surface so he had to climb up onto this to close it. You can only begin to imagine Richard in his orange fleece, underpants and skinny legs (which he assured me had been much admired in his Thespian days) clambering amongst the coffee, biscuits and other debris. Oh, to have been there with my video camera!

Bronco had told us before we left that we would really appreciate the hut on our return, and once again I had to eat my words as the hut was so inviting after our two nights by the ice despite me having pooh-poohed Bronco before our departure. First things first, on went the kettle for a brew and Bronco went off for a wash with his bucket of hot water from the kettle (now why hadn't I thought of that before?). Once that was done, Alison and I decided that before we washed, we would go out and collect the last of our water samples and carry out one of my minor objectives. I had promised a friend (who we called ickle Al, on account of his being vertically challenged) I would build him a snowman and photograph it for him and time was beginning to run out.

Once done, we headed back to Gruntly and Charmless for a wash before going up to the Russian hut for a party that evening. Feeling absolutely disgustingly filthy (and looking it too), Alison and Siaron decided to run the gauntlet and go and shower in the Chilean gym. Coward that I am, I hung back saying I'd wait to see how they got on before going. They came back looking so pleased with themselves that the temptation became too much for me and I thought I might just sneak in too. Oh, the bliss of a proper shower and hair wash – forget a weekend of pampering at Champneys, this beat it hands down for complete luxury. Just as I was about to leave, I heard a tennis ball being hit against a wall and with my heart in my mouth, I snuck out of the door and peeked into the hall to see who was there. Just my luck – the Chilean base commander who seriously disapproved of women being here much less in his gym from which we had been banned. Having gone back into the showers and realised that, of course, there weren't going to be any windows for me to climb out of, I had two remaining options. Brazen it out and stroll nonchalantly through the gym calling out 'Hola!' as I went, or try to escape unnoticed. Being the coward that I am, I opted for the crawl out on hands and knees option. So, like the Blues Brother trying to evade the police before getting to the ballroom to sing at their charity event, I dashed between pillars and eventually escaped through the doors to freedom.

JFDI

Preparing for the glacier walk

The team on the glacier

Whale bone on the shore

Camping near the glacier

The walk back to base

Ice in the bay back at base after the storm

Antarct-ickle Al snowman for my friend Al

Chapter 9

Russian Revelations

'Do not judge by appearances; a rich heart may be under a poor coat.'
Scottish proverb

The others left for the party, leaving me to write up and send the daily report back to the UK, and I then picked my way up the hillside to the Ryazan hut to join in the festivities. We were absolutely blown away by their hospitality. They had been fishing for us that afternoon and had rolled out the metaphorical red carpet and even broken out some precious stores of vodka they had secreted up there. The hut was heartbreaking – they had nothing and I almost sobbed as I went into their kitchen and they proudly showed me their drinks cabinet, shelves full of empty bottles. In their lounge they had no curtains, but one creative soul had used the tapes from cassettes and made beautiful swags and tails. Only one of them could speak English to any reasonable standard and he translated for us throughout the evening as he explained to us their backgrounds.

These were truly amazing people. Many of them were highly qualified people, but because of perestroika they had no chance of getting any work at home. For the princely sum of $4.50 a day (£3.00), they boarded a ship in Russia and sailed most of the way round the world to spend six months breaking up scrap metal. Compare this to the Chileans who were on the equivalent of $33 a day, and who would be able to go home and buy a house at the end of their 13-month stint! It then dawned on us why the Russians never socialised with the other bases – they didn't have the money or ability to entertain in return, not because they were miserable, anti-social so-and-sos.

Having got the biographies out of the way, they produced a guitar and started singing us home-grown Russian songs. We didn't need to understand the words to know they were about great hardship and overcoming great obstacles. Then it was our turn to sing some songs, but unfortunately between us, we didn't know one song all the way through. The best we could do was a badly tortured part rendition of *The Wild Rover*!

Before the evening finished, we had one final surprise. One of the men had carved us small penguins, all beautifully painted and mounted on stands (which still has pride of place on my dresser all these years later). More lumps in the throat and much hugging and back slapping as we staggered off into the near dark, feeling completely humbled by these great men. Having being bolstered by vodka, Chris had foolishly agreed to get up a six the next morning to go swimming with the Russians in the lake. I only wish I could have managed to pull myself out of bed in time to go and film it.

Unfortunately, I awoke the next morning having caught the cold which had been going around and was feeling pretty rough. I felt very guilty as the team went out to go and start clearing up the waste at the meteorological hut. When I finally dragged myself out of bed, I could see these tiny figures on the hillside shovelling the waste into sandbags. This was the by-product of making helium to send up the weather balloons when they had run out of stocks. Consequently, there was a huge slick of white gunge slicked down the hillside and they ran out of sandbags a long time before any real impact was made on it.

However, the Russians could finally begin to see that change was possible and the morale in the camp had improved dramatically since we arrived and it left them motivated to continue the good work.

In the meantime, Richard had gone out into the bay to take some depth measurements to take back to Buenos Aires to give to the company supplying the ship that would come to remove the waste. This then got transcribed onto a relatively accurate map that I managed to draw. Lunch followed and then, whilst standing in the lounge in the food hut, I looked out and caught an eye boggling sight. One of the Russians was walking down to the shore wearing just an anorak and flip flops. He shrugged off the jacket to reveal a rather small pair of Speedos, marched through the ice blocking the bay and went for a dip in the sea. And they talk about mad dogs and Englishmen going out in the midday sun!

The afternoon was spent collecting lichens. In the absence of any instructions, I just collected the same species in a line heading away from the base to see if they could assess any changes due to human habitation.

On our ice walk, I had picked up a couple of bits of driftwood and decided on my return to the hut to try and make a Mission Antarctic plaque to give to the Russians and the Uruguayans to thank them for their hospitality. Having spent a very happy hour, I got the Mission Antarctica Compass carved and painted and then asked everyone to sign them.

Armed with one of them, we got our lift back up to Artigas for our final Uruguayan party. It was pretty much a re-run of the first except with Pisco – some lethal Uruguayan concoction guaranteed to blow your socks off. I hadn't known how to go about giving the plaque to Waldemar, the base commander, so I took aside Hugo, one of the flight engineers, who was the spitting image of Danny DeVito and just as funny, to ask him. He was so moved by what I'd done, he immediately gave me his necklace before switching the lights off in the main room and introducing me. In extremely bad Spanish, I thanked the base commander for his hospitality. He responded in kind and then thankfully, that was that and it was back to dancing.

It was a very cosmopolitan affair, as a contingent of Chileans turned up along with some Italian glaciologists whom we had ever only spotted in the distance. They spent most of their days lowering themselves on ropes into caves under the glaciers – mad, mad, mad!

Eventually it was time to go home and it took a while to round everyone up. We finally got back only to make ourselves extremely unpopular with Richard (never a good thing) as the Uruguayans started tooting their horn and shouting goodbye to us at three in the morning.

JFDI

Emperor penguin carving

The UK team with the Russian team

Chapter 10

Soggy Farewells

'How lucky I am having something that makes saying goodbye so hard.'
A. A. Milne, *Winnie the Pooh*

Our penultimate day on the island started even slower than after the last party at Artigas and it was a day of tying up loose ends. Alison and I finally bagged up all the lichens and syringes and finished up the report before joining the others in putting together the goody bags for the Russians for the party we were hosting that night.

I was determined to give a better speech to the Russians than I had to the Uruguayans and persuaded the base doctor to help me translate a couple of sentences into Russian. He'd tried to do the same for Bronco, but unfortunately Bronco had to give up on the basis that he was incomprehensible whereas I managed, just, to pass muster.

The afternoon was a bit messy – the Uruguayans had half promised to take some of the girls up in the helicopter, so there was a lot of to-ing and fro-ing with many false starts and ultimately not being able to go.

The rest of us decided to go down to the Chinese base to try and get to talk to them having finally arranged a time the week before. On our arrival, they decided they couldn't see us after all, and added insult to injury as we smelt the glorious smells of Chinese food being cooked just feet away from where we stood. We consoled ourselves instead with buying a few knick-knacks from their souvenir shop and walked back again.

On returning we went down to the food mess and put up balloons and streamers and cracked out the bottles of champagne and wine before we started partying all over again. The chef had pulled out all the stops that night and had cooked chicken and chips. These had to be the most god-awful chips I had ever seen, looking more like limp maggots. But chips is chips and even I managed to swallow down a few.

I have never seen so much excitement in a group of people as I had with the Russians. They were allowed to drink alcohol for the first time in months and as the evening wore on, they got increasingly loud and excitable.

Bronco kicked off the speeches, translated by the doctor, and thus began a long stream of replies, first from

Oleg, the camp commander, then me with my plaque. A brief halt for photos was taken for the offending bit of wood, then Nat got up and presented a carved wooden elephant picture, and Oleg stood up again and gave Nat a certificate declaring him to be the first person from Thailand to visit the base. Maxim, a Russian scientist, then stood up, followed by the Italians, then Bronco announcing the gifts, then another Russian female scientist got up giving a lovely speech about the protection of the subspecies of humans that inhabit the Antarctic. Finally, the Italians stood up again to thank Igor for transporting them everywhere!

At that point, an accordion appeared for more tortured Russian songs (accompanied by tortured accordion playing) until a fed-up young gun came back with his tape machine and it was Russian disco time! With the male/female imbalance, in order to prevent riots a system involving a balloon was devised whereby all the men got to dance with the women. Whoever wanted to dance with a woman came up to the man who was already dancing with her and hit him on the head with said balloon. The woman was then given up to the balloon hitter and the balloon was passed on. Who would have thought that a simple balloon could cause so much entertainment? The next morning, there were definitely some sore heads around and still quite a few drunk Russians, who'd been so overexcited, they'd stayed up the whole night.

And then there it was, the final day – Valentine's Day no less and I was feeling pretty miserable as I really did not want to go home at all. Richard, on the other hand, was beside himself with excitement. Bronco had radioed the ship which was aiming to be with us by 6pm that evening and Richard had put his order in for gin and tonic to be served as soon as he set foot back on-board. He couldn't wait to get off what he called 'this godforsaken island'.

My misery was compounded by a visit to the Shop Russian – yet another case for the Trade Descriptions Act – to buy some stamps and other bits. As I arrived at the hut, Alison followed me in and was greeted with great gusto by the still drunk Russian meteorologist. He then repeated his effusive greetings to Alex and all the while I stood there being ignored. I must have given him the Espley death stare because he finally caught sight of me and flinched saying, 'Oh those eyes, so hard, like a cobra'. I'd already been told by the Uruguayans that I was like a mother, looking after everyone as well as being the team joker, which is all very well, but not when it would have been nice to have been seen as something other than court jester just once. Given my rather fragile ego particularly around men, it was as much as I could do to make my purchases before stumbling out and running back to the hut to the sanctuary of my sleeping platform. Quietly sobbing, I realised that I could escape to the end of the world, but I couldn't escape from me. I was still putting up barriers that meant people saw me in a certain way no matter how open and friendly I thought I was being. It was a very sobering moment for me.

My mood was lightened when we took the team photos and one of the meteorologists, William, popped over from the Chilean base and offered to take me round. I spent a very pleasant hour in his company as he showed what he did. It was rounded up by a visit to their mess. Once again, I was agog – they had proper bedrooms with proper beds and a dining area at which a waiter (yes, really!) was laying a table for lunch with linen and silver cutlery in preparation for some five-course lunch. It was unbelievable that this place existed, where two hundred yards down the beach, we were sleeping on floors and dining on dried apricot. My illusions about being chosen to come on the walk with him were soon shattered when I realised he was asking rather a lot about Alison and swiftly took up my offer of a return visit to our hut when he established that she was going to be there. I was the convenient and safe route in.

I could put off packing no longer and we all knuckled down to clearing up Gruntly and filling the barrels with what we were taking back with us. Having dusted and swept out the hut and piled our rucksacks in the lounge, there was nothing left to do. Igor was supposed to be turning up at 3pm with the truck to shift all the gear back down to the beach but never appeared. Every time Bronco stalked off to find him, the answer was always 'soon'. This is a very flexible term in Russian and means anywhere from one hour to three days!

On the basis that in this case 'soon' wasn't likely to be, we all wandered off, lost in our private thoughts about leaving. I took my diary and cigarettes and headed up to the cliffs and sat there for a couple of hours. I just sat there trying to imprint as much of the surroundings onto my brain and thinking about the last few weeks. What struck me, as I sat there and looked down at the Chilean and Russian base, was the complete lack of people. Whilst there were around 70 people between both bases, you rarely saw one or two of them at any one time. What were they all doing? Finally, the biting wind got the better of me and I could see the truck crawling its way to the hut, so I reluctantly left my post and wandered back over to Gruntly for the last time.

It was at that moment the Russians decided to finally come and empty our toilet – just a week too late, lads! As the last bag went on to the truck and we bid a farewell to our little home, Eduardo from Artigas came screaming over in a truck and handed out notes to us. The Uruguayans had promised to come down and wave us off, but unfortunately, they had been called away to another base and wouldn't make it back in time.

I had one small heart-warming moment which I cherish to this day. I have mentioned the Italian glaciologists and one of them was rather attractive. I was chatting to him standing on the balcony outside the mess and we were talking about how the Uruguayans had been courting the other ladies. I think I must have looked rather sad because he turned to me and said they were blind and that still waters ran deep with me. I was so delighted that someone (particularly so charming and handsome) had seen past my rather prickly exterior.

Returning indoors, we sat down for one last meal and sat around chatting until one of us saw the boat and we all ran out to have a look at the tiny speck out in the bay. Far too soon, it took shape, anchored out in the bay and before we knew it, Jonas had arrived on the beach in the Zodiac ready to take us away. We all clambered into our wet weather gear and I walked down following everyone to the boat filming our last moments. How different our departure was to our arrival! From brooding and silent when we arrived, the Russians were now whooping and cheering us and the doctor was in tears with the departure of his best pal Richard. It was all too much. In the Zodiac, Siaron sat opposite me with tears streaming down her face and I couldn't bear to intrude on her grief and film it (much to Richard's disgust). We waved and waved and shouted goodbye until they could hear us no longer and turned to face the ship.

No sooner had we bumped alongside than Richard had scrambled off and leapt gazelle-like up the gangway, having spotted Elke and the promised gin and tonic. We were also far too excited so rather than go and shower, which had been an earlier major priority, we instead headed straight to the bar for a drink and catch-up with the crew. Quite what the new guests on-board thought of this smelly group of overexcited people, we never knew. One minute they were enjoying a civilised dinner with celebratory Valentine's cake, and the next were rudely interrupted by rowdy chattering and raucous laughter.

Siaron and I disappeared on deck to watch the receding lights of the base and to wave at the Korean base where we knew the Uruguayans were, our hearts full, not quite believing it was all over.

Then it was back to the ship routine and the joy that was the tannoy system. I was very pleased to hear that there had been a near mutiny over it on this trip from the other passengers, so much so that the next morning we were spared it. Sadly, it was our only day of relief and it was back to situation normal after that. The next two days were uneventful for me as I lay prostrate in my cabin fighting off seasickness again. Very dull and boring but lying down was the only way to keep my stomach under control.

On the plus side, it gave me plenty of thinking time. The trip had crystallised many unformed thoughts. I realised that I didn't want to spend the rest of my life chained to a desk. I had felt immense satisfaction from carrying out the research for so many reasons; being able to just get on with it at my own pace, yet being able to finish it on time, working outdoors for part of it had been a major plus, and not having someone breathing down my neck telling me I could do it better. I loved the alternative lifestyle – there was such a raw vibrancy about it all. Maybe it was the language barrier, or the location, or being female in such places, but there was an honesty about it that I liked.

People say what they mean – sooner and with greater clarity so you are left in no doubt. Even Mr Cobra – as much as it hurt, at least I knew exactly how he felt! It had an end of the world feel about it and not in the geographical sense, more of a grasping the here and now and tomorrow will sort itself out. Maybe I was a frontierswoman in a previous life!

I knew then that I could not stay at Standard Life and be true to myself.

Bronco was very understanding and said that it was the same kind of feeling that you get on expeditions. I had a long chat with him about how I could get back to Bellingshausen and we batted around some ideas.

My mental perambulations aside, we were very fortunate again with the weather and made such good time that we arrived at Cape Horn several hours ahead of schedule and had to hang around waiting for the signal from the pilot that we could come down the Beagle Channel. You hear such dreadful stories about Cape Horn, but it was hard to imagine it that day. The sun shone, the skies were blue and the swell not much more than a gentle undulation.

Our last night on-board was pretty wild and ended with us dancing in the kitchens in the bowels of the ship with some of the crew, drinking copious amounts of Irish coffee and dancing around the ovens!

We eventually arrived back at Ushuaia very early in the morning and feeling rather shabby, we decamped to a small pension, the Posada, for our debrief. Bronco prodded us in the right mental direction and we put together our action plans for when we returned to the UK. Once that was out of the way, we went for lunch at the Tolkeyen Hotel, a beautiful hotel on the shoreline past the airport. Bronco had us howling with laughter as he ordered 'aqua con leche'. He had meant carbonated water but had got his 'con gaz' mixed with his 'con leche' and the waiter looked suitably bemused as he wondered why anyone would want milk with their water!

In amongst all this, I was trying to fulfil a mysterious assignment given to me by Richard. The previous night, I had been dragged off to his cabin and told that he wanted me to go and film Ushuaia. My objective being to make him understand what it was all about and to make him laugh. It was a tall order, and although he wouldn't tell me what it was about, I could sense it was important.

So from early dawn and throughout the day, I filmed what I thought was the essence of Ushuaia and spent three and a half happy hours wandering through the shanty towns filming at will. This essence seemed to consist mostly of lupins, dogs, triangular huts, Christmas decorations not taken down, broken pavements, and not forgetting the imposing mountain peaks behind Ushuaia. I found it quite hard to try and film people going about their business without being too intrusive, whilst wanting to capture their day to day lives too.

Then it was back down to the port to say goodbye to the *Vavilov* and the crew who were off again across the Passage less than 12 hours from having docked earlier that morning. They must be exhausted after a whole season of that. It was very sad to wave them off as the *Vavilov* had become like a second home to us.

Back at the Posada, I nervously handed my tapes over to Richard for editorial proofing. Richard, bless him, couldn't keep a secret and before long had admitted that he had suggested to Bronco that I go as the film person on the next year's trip to the Antarctic as part of the 44 from 44 expedition, where 44 young expeditioners from 44 countries sail to Bellingshausen to see the rubbish being removed. He swore me to secrecy and to leave it to him and Bronco to try and organise.

I was so excited at the thought of getting back to the Antarctic, even knowing it would be very different from this trip. I felt more focused and energised about my life than I had in a long time. I wasn't even sure at that moment if my thoughts of becoming a freelance consultant was the way forward – my diary entry ends that day with 'Expeditions are go!'

The next day we flew back to Buenos Aires and almost baked in the heat of the place, our clothing being entirely unsuited to the tropical heat. All my clothes were so rancid, they all went directly to the laundry other than for a pair of tracksuit bottoms and a top needed for a wander around the city. Dinner was taken at an Irish pub and I had the best steak I have ever tasted in my life. I treated myself to an early night and awoke to a power cut which caused barked shins and much cursing whilst trying to dress in the pitch black when I couldn't work out how to open the shutters.

Having had the most delicious breakfast, I began filming the end of trip interviews with everyone. Bronco had me weeping once again with his malapropisms. He'd wanted to talk about how he felt this trip had vindicated all the work that was being done at Bellingshausen. Having had his practice, I started filming him and he started talking about how he felt mitigated at the work. I had to stop him the second time he used 'mitigated' and ask him if that was really what he wanted to say. He collapsed with laughter, demanded a cigarette and then got ready for the next take. He got vindicated out OK this time, but unfortunately caught my face which was twitching with suppressed laughter and that was it, he crumbled again! Eventually he decided that the only way this was going to work was to look directly to the camera rather than to me and we finally had success on the third take.

With an afternoon to fritter away before catching our flight, we all disappeared off. I went and sat at a café and wrote down my thoughts and a list of top tips for the next year's group to go into an overall document on the expedition that I had offered to put together.

At the airport we bid our soggy farewells to Richard and Bronco, who were staying on to finalise plans for the ship for the following year.

The flight back was your normal run-of-the-mill flights – sit on the tarmac for an hour before departure, earphones and overhead lights that don't work, full to the gunwales and a very reassuring message from the captain telling the cabin crew to take their seats for landing before we'd even departed! I was determined that come what may, I was going to sleep on the plane and knowing that the two Nytol I'd taken on the way out hadn't worked, I took three. What a mistake to make! I got a restless leg and nothing I did eased it. I spent what felt like hours marching up and down the aisle or trying to sleep with my leg raised on the seat in front of me, convinced I'd overdosed and was about to have a stroke. I finally collapsed into a coma about an hour before landing at Gatwick and woke up feeling like a zombie. Which was not a great feeling considering we'd been warned we might be having a press conference once we cleared customs. Strangely (at the time), Standard Life had vetoed it and it was only later that we realised in our absence some carpetbagger had raised a motion to demutualise the company and they hadn't wanted us to inadvertently say anything damaging (even though we hadn't a clue – we had been stuck in the Antarctic after all!).

There were a few people waiting for us when we staggered out of customs. I don't know how the others felt, but I was completely bewildered and was on the verge of tears – it really was all over now. I have to assume the others felt the same way as we all milled around aimlessly, lost without Bronco to guide us.

My good friend and ex brother-in-law, James, had come to meet me and sensibly he organised me and tore me away from my daydreaming and hustled me towards the car that Standard Life had laid on for us. We got taken to a hotel to give us a night of luxury before heading back to normality and it was a welcome touch. They also delivered a bouquet of flowers and a bottle of champagne which I really couldn't face as I was still feeling like a space cadet after my Nytol. Instead, James took me down to Brighton for the afternoon where I wandered around completely bemused and feeling like an alien from another planet.

After a good meal and a great night's sleep, James drove me home and I had the weekend to sort myself out before going back to work. I spent a lot of time thinking about what I'd be doing if I was still in the Antarctic. Saturday night was party night at Artigas and there I was in Surrey, filling up the washing machine and opening four weeks' worth of post. But like any memorable trip, you remember only the good times and I was excited to share my tales with many people at Standard Life to help keep the memories alive. And it was now time to start giving some serious thought to the future and if I was going to be brave enough to make changes.

JFDI

Chinese base (Great Wall) on King George Island

The Russians enjoying their first drinks at the farewell party

*The handing over of the driftwood
Mission Antarctica plaque*

Finally emptying our loo!

Back at Cape Horn, all lost in thought

Chapter 11

Reality Bites

'She might be down to earth and rooted in reality and by her responsibilities, but her soul is a wild one; always set on finding magic in sunsets and sunrises that others take for granted.'

Daniel Mercury, *Love Her Right*

It was rather surreal going back to work. I was immediately thrown back into the thick of the project I had been on before I left. I'd secretly hoped to come back to a bit of a hero's welcome – the return of the intrepid and daring explorer showered in ticker tape and rapturous applause as I walked through the doors. But apart from a few brief chats with people who'd been reading my emails, my reappearance barely created a ripple and within hours, it felt like I'd never been gone. The magic and euphoria of my trip evaporated.

On one hand, it would have been quite nice to bask in the glory of being an intrepid explorer for a little while, but I suppose it gave me very little time to brood on my time away and I probably adjusted back into 'real life' far quicker than I might otherwise have. Still, I would have appreciated at least a small flurry of ticker tape.

The next two months were spent in a frenzy of trying to prepare the business for the new claims system, ensuring all the training material was prepared and usable, carrying out user acceptance testing, working out how to prove that the system did what it needed to do, grappling with the many permutations of the new letter system, writing the implementation weekend plan, appeasing the directors, and wondering if today was the day when I lost the plot completely.

I don't think I had one day off the entire month as weekends were spent in testing and gathering the key data to prove everything was working as expected. The hysteria was almost too much to bear and things only got worse when my test manager left me high and dry having decided to take another contract elsewhere.

It was only a matter of time before somebody fell off their perch and given that I had been given an award for 'Person most stressed on the project' at a Christmas do, I was pretty much a front runner in that department. I was very relieved when it ended up being one of the external consultants who had been working herself up into a frenzy and it all became too much for her seven days before blast off. I was quietly delighted because she'd been constantly on my case with her perfect checklists and professional ways and we'd been secret rivals. Her going down gave me a real boost as I realised I was made of sterner stuff after all and I knew I was going to survive.

Suddenly, everything came together. The results were in and I presented them to the Board and senior IT managers at the weekly debrief, showing them that all things being equal, the baby would fly. There was a bit of a stunned moment when they realised that somehow, I'd managed to pull the equivalent of a rabbit out of a hat and that after all the chaos, I had done what I had set out to achieve. Realisation dawned that they had probably misjudged me – my Pig Pen approach to project management actually did work. OK, so I wasn't obsessed with project management plans and it was sometimes quite difficult for others to understand exactly where everything was, but they should have trusted that once the dust settled around me, I would deliver as required.

There was a further manic two weeks preparing for the system to go live and then managing all the snagging problems once it had been given to the front line staff. But we'd done it. After all that time, £12m and unbelievable pressure, we'd only bloody done it!

Espley pulls it off!

Life returned to some semblance of normality and bar the tidying up of loose ends, everything settled down. Which then allowed me the breathing space to ask the big question – what next?

They wanted me to carry on with the roll out of the system to the rest of the customer care teams or, if I preferred, I could return to Provider Services and pick up the reins there.

I had a third choice, and that was to leave the company…

So I had to make a decision. Should I stay or should I go? Bearing in mind that I had been working consistently for 20 years at this point and been in the health insurance/ corporate land for 15 of those years, this was not a decision to be made lightly.

There was safety in staying – I'd covered myself in glory and had not only managed to deliver a new claims system, but had set up a team in Provider Services that was delivering great value to the business. But… I felt like I'd done what I could in Provider Services and I'm not a Forth Bridge kinda person. Doing the same things day after day doesn't excite me. New and shiny (and apparently stress) does. And both options for staying at Standard Life felt rather like doing the same old same old.

One thing I had been terribly disappointed about was what happened next with our Mission Antarctica trip. Part of our remit was that we would go around Standard Life talking about our trip and what we'd learned and to share our experiences. This had all been cancelled thanks to the carpetbagger which was such a shame because I could talk for hours about my time there and it felt like a lost opportunity to spread the story about protecting the environment.

With that gone, there really didn't feel like there was anything for me to stay for. But to give it all up without a firm plan of what I was going to do next was also extremely scary.

I had to keep reminding myself that my FOF had matured. I now had enough money saved to last me a year without worrying about whether I could survive without work. And this was the whole point of it. To give me options, to enable me to test the world outside of the safety of a good job in a large organisation, and to prove to myself that I could escape the cage of expectations and (whispers it) start to live life on my terms. Crazy talk!

Looking back on it now, I am amazed that I had the courage to leave, but somewhere inside me, the pioneer stood up and persuaded me of the possibilities. I resigned and after working my notice period, I walked away from corporate life to who knows what.

JFDI

Chapter 12

Turning the Page

'Girls you've gotta know when it's time to turn the page.'
Tori Amos, *Northern Lad*, from the album *From the Choirgirl Hotel*

My parents were horrified, of course. This was not the behaviour they expected and they were terrified for my future. They sent me job advert after job advert in the hope I would come to my senses and go back to having a safe job in a large company. They simply could not understand that there might be a different way to live your life. I get it – in their day, you worked, you retired, you died. Simple. You did not do anything to upset the apple cart or try to plough your own furrow.

Amazingly, I stuck to my guns and despite me continuing in my search for enlightenment all these years later and other than a brief stint as a marketing director for a much smaller company, I never went back to full-time employment in the corporate world.

After the mania of the last few months I was completely exhausted and burned out, so I slept a lot and allowed myself to do nothing. It's funny; you think you'll catch up on your sleep and one day you'll feel energised again. But in fact, the opposite happened. It turns out it's actually incredibly tiring doing nothing.

My world became increasingly nocturnal as I had longer and later lie-ins, but then not sleeping at the other end of the day until the early hours. After several weeks of this, I decided things had to change when it was mid-afternoon and I was still in my dressing gown, having achieved nothing more constructive than to eat breakfast.

Time to get the thinking cap on and make a plan of action. I realised there were two things I wanted to do. First, to see if I could make it as a freelance consultant and secondly, to explore either getting back to the Antarctic or looking at alternative lifestyles.

I have always been good at staying in touch with people when I moved jobs – I tried not to burn any bridges when I left. Particularly in the health insurance industry, you never know when you might meet someone again in a different role, so telling them what you really thought of them, was not a great strategy.

Not that there were many I'd liked to have vent my spleen at. Generally, I'd met and become friends with a large number of people on the way. But there are always a few bad apples along the way who try to make your life a misery and you wish you could find a way to say something to save others from suffering later.

I wrote to lots of my old contacts telling them I had left Standard Life and was available to support them if they had any suitable roles. Incredibly it worked and I had a constant flow of short-term contracts which suited my love of shiny new things to a T. And it showed me that I was pretty versatile and able to pick up new things and run with them well. My equivalent of my apprenticeship grown from starting off life as a humble admin assistant through to managing a £12million project over 15 years, had equipped me well with a broad range of experience.

I'd also stayed in touch with Bronco who got me involved with an outdoor team building company (Action Based Leadership) and I enjoyed a fabulous experience with him and a colleague of his, putting some graduates for one of the large city banks through their paces before they started their training.

And then I got a call from Richard, the cameraman from our trip, telling me about a really exciting project. He, along with another film-maker, had been asked to film the unveiling of a memorial in Arromanches in France and they needed a third member of the crew to help with supplemental filming.

In the latter stages of the war, great floating harbours were to be built on the coast of north France code-named 'Mulberry B'. One at Arromanches (also known as Port Winston) was to be assembled and operated by men of the Royal Engineers (Transportation) under the command of Brigadier A.E.M. Walter CBE, Royal Engineers at Arromanches. Before that though, they had to land on the beaches of Normandy, in what became known as the D-Day landings.

The floating harbour was hugely pivotal in the ending of the war. More than 2.5 million men, 500,000 vehicles and 4 million tonnes of supplies arrived via Port Winston in the ten months after D-Day. But for some reason their actions had never been recognised. Finally, by 2000, money had been raised and a trip had been organised to take the veterans across the channel to take part in several days of activities, culminating in the unveiling of the memorial and attending a gala dinner.

And so it was, that I found myself on a coach in Reading, surrounded by veterans of the Second World War, heading to Dover and across to France where we, along with Lady Mary Soames (Winston Churchill's daughter) would thank them their wartime efforts for this incredible achievement. My job was to talk to the men and hopefully video some of their stories for posterity, whilst Richard and Michael had gone ahead to scout locations.

The trip to France was rather lovely – the men were all excited about the trip and on the ferry we all got upgraded to luxury class because Lady Soames was with us, so the trip started on a high.

It's too easy to dismiss the older generation as being out of touch with their, to us, old fashioned ways and their increased frailty. But my goodness, were my eyes opened over those few days!

Their bravery and valour would put most of us today to shame. What they endured in the name of their country was mind-boggling. Not only did they have to land on the beaches under fire watching many of their comrades being shot and killed, but they then had to build and maintain the floating pontoons.

Having built the pontoons, the area was struck by a massive five-day storm (from the 19th to 25th June 1944). It was only thanks to this intrepid group of men that the floating harbour at Arromanches survived, when others along the coast sank.

I spoke to one chap who was knee-high to a grasshopper and he explained to me that in the height of the storm they'd strapped themselves to the pontoon and 'wanked the anchors' (his words, not mine!), meaning that they worked the anchor ropes to allow the pontoons to stay afloat amidst the storm waves.

We took the group on various trips to visit old war sites and beaches where some of them had landed. I remember going to one beach and Richard's colleague, Michael (who was an ex rugby player and built like a sh*t brick outhouse), was down at the beach interviewing one of the veterans about his landing. All we could see from our position about a hundred yards away was Michael suddenly doubling over and staggering away. He ran up to me in floods of tears, thrust the camera into my hands asking me to take over and walked off, sobbing.

The chap he'd been speaking to had talked about the horrors of the landing, how he'd had to come ashore wading through blood-drenched seas and having to push past the dead bodies of his comrades. And how it then contrasted with the glorious day, with the sun shining and families playing in the sand enjoying themselves and wondering how different it might have been had he and his comrades not been successful. But also saying that was why they'd done what they did – they felt it was their duty to sacrifice themselves (if needs be) to protect future generations. It was incredibly moving.

At last the day for the big unveiling of the plaque arrived. I was to film the men marching into the square and round to the front. They were all dressed in their best with their medals shining in the evening sun, all holding themselves upright and proud, along with their French counterparts. The band started playing and the men started singing as they slowly marched around the square. I'm welling up writing this nearly 20 years later – I can't tell you how moving it was. How I managed to film it without the camera shaking is nobody's business.

The evening was rounded off with a gala dinner at which the Brigadier, at 92 years old, stood up ramrod straight and gave a rousing speech. I went and spoke to him afterwards and it turned out that he had flown in from Perth, Australia for the event! He'd only emigrated there about six years previously and stoutly declared he wished he'd done it sooner.

Honestly, they don't make men like that anymore. My heart was bursting with pride that I'd been able to witness heroism and stoicism in the face of such adversity. And we complain these days about having to wear a mask!

By the following day, I'd come down with lurgy, but had to rustle everyone back on the coach for our return trip, whilst Richard and Michael finished off in France. I felt shockingly unwell and it was made far worse when we got back on the ferry. The veterans naturally headed to first class as that's where they'd been on the way out. Unfortunately, the bursar wasn't having any of it and because we no longer had Lady Soames with us, they were all dispatched down to steerage again. I was apoplectic with rage. My entreaties fell on deaf ears and no amount of explaining what these men had done and that this journey was probably the last one for many of them made the slightest jot of difference. The bursar didn't even offer free drinks by way of at least demonstrating some humanity – his computer definitely said no! For shame! It's so important for us all to be reminded of the sacrifices people have made for our freedom.

We need to learn from our older generations – they have such stories to tell and they deserve our respect. I learned that valuable lesson from that remarkable group of men.

I apologised profusely to them, but they merely looked sad and resigned to the usual treatment old folk get. I sat out on the deck wrapped up against the cold, crying about the unfairness of it all and wishing I could have done something to make a difference.

I never got paid for those three days; Richard and Michael spent the money before they could give me any, but whilst I was slightly aggrieved, they offered me an experience I will never forget and I shall be ever grateful for that.

Within six months of having left Standard Life, I'd had a range or experiences that showed me that there were real alternatives to being a corporate wage slave. And that allowed me to realise I had choices on how to live my life and that I could flourish in this new world.

I realised that I am immensely adaptable and that I loved work that allowed me to be really practical and hands-on. And had room for creativity.

In my other quest to get back to the Antarctic, I wanted to investigate ways that I could build my experience of working with youth. And I looked into doing Voluntary Service Oversees, but that was a two-year commitment which felt a long time if it turned out it wasn't for me. I needed to find a way to test the waters before leaping into something that would be such a dramatic change but that might not be right for me.

Fortunately, Bronco turned up trumps again and put me in touch with Sue Stockdale.

Sue is another of life's incredible people.

In 1994, she became the first British woman to ski to the Magnetic North Pole where she faced temperatures cold enough to freeze your flesh in seconds. She has also participated in expeditions to the Geographic North Pole, Greenland and Antarctica; and has travelled to over 70 countries. She is now a motivational speaker, executive coach and delivers leadership development programmes. She is another hero of mine.

Sue very kindly agreed to meet me and off I went to a small village in Oxfordshire where she talked to me about her experiences with Operation Raleigh (now called Raleigh International). It is a not-for-profit organisation with the mission of 'Inspiring communities and young people around the world to create lasting change'. They organise expeditions to a variety of countries around the world, taking young people between the age of 17 and 24. They typically tend to be a mixture of gap year students, along with youth at risk (young people who may be homeless or addicts), and they visit these countries to take part in three main activities – an environmental project, a community project and finally, a personal development activity (a three-week trek). The participants experience different cultures, meet new people and help improve communities through building schools or latrine blocks. As someone (well) over the age of 24, I would be looking at going as a volunteer manager where I would be helping to develop and support the venturers, as they are called. It seemed like the perfect solution for me – I could get my experience working with youth, I would be working outdoors and have another 'adventure'. As it was only a three-month commitment, it would give me a good flavour of that sort of life and if it turned out it wasn't for me, then at least it was only three months.

With Sue's encouragement, I applied to go on a Raleigh expedition. How my life changed in the short space of 12 months! All because I was offered an opportunity to go to the Antarctic, an experience which changed me forever.

Finally, at the age of 37, I had the courage to stand up for what I wanted, rather than bending to the will of others. It might have happened in any case – I had after all been putting money into my FOF before I knew about the Antarctic expedition. But I suspect it may have taken a little longer to have the courage to do so without the catalyst of a trip that opened up a world I didn't know existed, let alone could exist in.

It made me realise that I wanted to create a life that worked for me. A life which played to my strengths of being practical and allowed me to be outdoors where I feel such freedom and vitality. It also awakened an inner calling to the environmental challenges we face, so I became a much more conscious consumer (and many years later, an anti-single use plastics activist).

The US Navy Seals have a saying that you eat an elephant one bite at a time. I still had plenty of gnarly elephant to eat, but at least I had started the journey. My journey of self-discovery seems to consist of two main threads. The trips gave me the challenge of a physically demanding adventure which had been missing from my life. And somehow the physical demands combined with a stripping back of life's luxuries, gave me some mental head space. They provided me time for reflection and some self-development, that I was unable to achieve in my day to day environment.

The next challenge with Raleigh International couldn't have been more different from the trip to Antarctica. I went from one extreme to another – from the ice and snow of the Antarctic Circle to the tropical heat of a West African country. But there were similarities in both expeditions. Both offered a much simpler lifestyle than I was used to, and I faced dangers in both, albeit that were very different in West Africa from the angry sea lions and skuas of the Antarctic to snakes and guns as two examples…

My three-month trip to Ghana gave me more time for reflection that I still desperately needed.

That trip also led to another, rather more extreme adventure – one that involved me, along with four other Raleigh staff, travelling back to the UK overland through West Africa, using only public transport. Something I would never have even thought of, let alone have had the courage to do, had I not had the Raleigh experience.

My trip to the Antarctic triggered a wonderful chain reaction of events with new doors opening up to me, taking me in all sorts of unfamiliar directions. I was entering uncharted territory and it was exciting.

If you are curious to find out about my Ghana adventures with a group of young adults facing challenging conditions, and antics that will make your eyes water, you won't have long to wait. My next book will reveal all…

JFDI

Glossary

Corporate Bollocks — as described by Karen, 'the politically back-stabbing, sabre rattling, gung-ho management world that seemed to be part and parcel of corporate life in the 80s and 90s'

FOF — F**k Off Fund

Imposter Syndrome — the persistent inability to believe that one's success is deserved or has been legitimately achieved as a result of one's own efforts or skills (O.E.D.)

JFDI — Just f***ing do it!

OSB — One Step Beyond, an environmental project set up by Robert Swan, with the aim to recycle and remove 1,500 tonnes of waste from Antarctica

PLU — People Like Us

Additional Information

Books I loved reading

In the Footsteps of Scott, Roger Mear, Robert Swan, Lindsay Fulcher, London: Jonathan Cape Ltd, 1987.

Covers their walk to the South Pole following Scott's route. There's also a fascinating section (Appendix 4) on the physiology of sustained and arduous exertion in Polar conditions.

Military Mountaineering: A History of Services Mountaineering 1945-2000, Bronco Lane, Hayloft, 2000.

A First Rate Tragedy: Captain Scott's Antarctic Expeditions, Diane Preston, Constable, 1997.

Another fascinating insight into the polar expedition and all the events and other trips the team took. And highlights the failings of the team compared with the Norwegian team led by Amundsen.

Mrs Chippy's Last Expedition, 1914-1915: The remarkable journal of Shackleton's polar-bound cat, Caroline Alexander, Bloomsbury, 1998.

A unique, humorous and poignant story on the ill-fated *Endurance* from the ship's cat's perspective.

Endurance: Shackleton's Incredible Voyage to the Antarctic, Alfred Lansing, Weidenfeld & Nicholson, 2000.

Other source information

Bronco Lane and Brummie Stokes' epic summiting of Everest where Bronco lost his fingertips and half his feet – an interview:
https://web.archive.org/web/20160604125205/http://www.everest1953.co.uk/michael-bronco-lane

The sinking of the Southern Quest – In the footsteps of Scott:
https://www.abc.net.au/news/2018-02-27/southern-quest-ship-sinking-off-antarctica-like-watching-titanic/9379558

Antarctic treaty 2041: https://2041foundation.org/

Jacques Cousteau mission:
https://www.temasek.com.sg/en/news-and-views/stories/sustainability/generational-investing/saving-antarctica-climate-change-robert-swan

Robert Swan - wikipedia:
https://en.wikipedia.org/wiki/Robert_Swan

Arromanches:
https://www.atlasobscura.com/places/mulberry-harbour-at-arromanches

https://www.arromanches-museum.com/ports/

https://www.thetimes.co.uk/article/grateful-town-where-d-day-veterans-are-treated-like-royalty-hnkz8mbw2

https://www.normandymemorialtrust.org/brochure/NMT-Brochure-English.pdf

Acknowledgements

I would never have had the courage to take the steps to get this book published without the prodding of my friends who urged me to get on with it. There are too many to mention by name, but I will shout out the Beaver Haven crew who have been a rock of support and a source of great laughter.

To Sara Hindhaugh, artist extraordinaire, who took my childish ideas for a book cover, completely turned them on their head and came up with something immensely better, which became the basis for the final version.

Thanks to Elliott Frisby of Monkeynut Audiobooks & Sound, who saw the potential in my draft copy and recommended me to a publishing company…

Thanks to the publishing team at Book Brilliance Publishing – to Olivia for helping me knock the book into shape, Zara for her fabulous typesetting skills, and Brenda for her on-going support and guidance throughout the process. And to Tammy for the final cover design.

I know I thank them in the book, but I must thank again Standard Life for giving me the opportunity to go to the Antarctic – I will be forever grateful for the best experience of my life.

And to Robert Swan who started it all off, Bronco Lane, my all-time hero, and Sue Stockdale, who continues to inspire me.

About the Author

After 15 years' working in large businesses, clawing her way up the greasy career ladder starting as an admin assistant, through to being the business manager on a £12m IT project, where she worked increasingly long hours with almost unbearable levels of stress, Karen realised there must be more to life.

Having had a life-changing trip to the Antarctic in 2000 and saved enough money to last a year, she took the plunge and began her journey to find a different way to live and to escape from the expectations she grew up with.

Karen worked in start-ups, businesses that failed, a business that grew from nothing to 150 employees that was then sold. She was an owner and shareholder of a successful consultancy practice, and has been a freelance consultant. In addition, she studied for an MBA to understand in more depth how business works. She's learned (sometimes painful) lessons and has helped many businesses grow using her broad experience and the lessons she's learned along the way. She has also published a book, *The Profitable Business*, to help small businesses grow and succeed.

Karen is widely travelled having had some epic journeys around the world, including West Africa, Australia and New Zealand as well as the Antarctic.

The Impulsive Explorer is the first of a trilogy about Karen's adventures; it will be followed by *The Curious Explorer* and *The Escaping Explorer*.

She lives in West Sussex with her two cats and is planning the next stage of her adventures.

Also by Karen Espley:

The Profitable Business

Coming Soon:

The Curious Explorer
The Escaping Explorer

Keep In Touch:
www.karenespley.com